Wonders

Practice Book

Mc
Graw
Hill

mheducation.com/prek-12

Send all inquiries to:
McGraw Hill
1325 Avenue of the Americas
New York, NY 10019

ISBN: 978-1-26-580516-6
MHID: 1-26-580516-4

Printed in the United States of America.

8 9 10 11 SMN 27 26 25 24 23

D

Contents

Week 5

Week 1

Week 2

Week 3

Week 4

Week 5

Week 1

Week 2

Week 3

Week 4

Week 5

Week 5

Copyright © McGraw Hill.

Week 5

Week 5

Name _____

Listen to the sounds your teacher says. Blend the sounds to make a word. Circle the picture that goes with that word.

1.

2.

3.

4.

5.

Teacher Directions: Model item 1 by saying: */k/ /a/ /b/ /i/ /n/. Listen as I blend these sounds: /kaaabiiinnn/, cabin. I see a picture that shows a cabin, so I will circle it.* Guide children to blend the sounds and circle the picture. For items 2-5, have children listen to the sounds, blend them to form a word, and circle the correct picture. 2. Say: /k/ /a/ /n/; 3. Say: /k/ /i/ /d/; 4. Say: /m/ /a/ /p/; 5. Say: /b/ /a/ /k/ /p/ /a/ /k/.

Name _____

Say the name of each picture. Say the middle sounds. Circle the picture whose name has a different middle sound.

Teacher Directions: Model item 1. Say: *Listen to the middle sounds of these words:* bat, cat, rip. Stress the difference between short vowel sounds /a/ and /i/. Say: *I hear that the words* bat *and* cat *have the same middle sound:* /a/. *The word* rip *has the middle sound* /i/. Guide children to circle the picture that goes with *rip*.

Name _____

The letter *a* can stand for the sound you hear in *fan*. The letter *i* can stand for the sound you hear in *bib*.

fan   *bib*

A. Circle the word that names each picture.

1.	big	2.	sit	3.	vet
	ban		lip		van
	bag		lap		man
4.	wag	5.	pack	6.	map
	win		kit		pat
	wig		kick		pit

B. Write the word that names the picture.

1. _____   2. _____

Name _____

Read the words. Listen for the short *a* or short *i* sound. Write the word that names each picture.

| bat   pig   cap   pin   napkin   zigzag |

1.  _____

2.  _____

3.  _____

4.  _____

5. 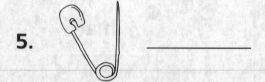 _____

6.  _____

Change one letter to make a new word with the short *a* or short *i* sound. Then write the word.

1. did _____

2. tap _____

3. hat _____

4. sick _____

Name _____

> A **plural noun** names more than one person, place, or thing.
> Add **-s** to form the plural noun for most words. Add **-es** to form
> the plural of nouns that end in **s**, **ss**, or **x**.

A. Write the plural form for each noun.

1. win _____   **2.** tag _____

3. tax _____   **4.** tip _____

5. pass _____   **6.** kiss _____

7. nap _____   **8.** gas _____

B. Look at the picture and write the word.

1.

2.   _____

Name _____

Read and spell the words in the box. Then identify which word completes the sentence.

ball	blue	both	even	for
help	put	there	why	yellow

1. I like _____ of my cats.

2. Can you _____ me fix this?

3. Jan has the _____ pen.

4. _____ are they sad?

5. Can you _____ the lid on this?

6. This is _____ you.

7. Do you like to play _____?

8. My dad has a _____ hat.

9. _____ are six pigs.

10. I like to play tag, _____ if I am sick.

Teacher Directions: Point to the word *ball*. Use the **Read/Spell/Write** routine. Repeat for each word in the box.

Name _____

Fold back the paper along the dotted line. Use the blanks to write each word as it is read aloud. When you finish the test, unfold the paper. Use the list at the right to correct any spelling mistakes.

Review Words

High-Frequency Words

1. _____
2. _____
3. _____
4. _____
5. _____
6. _____
7. _____
8. _____
9. _____
10. _____
11. _____
12. _____
13. _____
14. _____
15. _____

1. has
2. wag
3. bad
4. six
5. will
6. sat
7. had
8. fix
9. him
10. if
11. can
12. hit
13. why
14. for
15. help

Name _____

has	wag	bad	six	will
sat	had	fix	him	if

A. Write the spelling words that have the short *a* sound.

1. _____   4. _____

2. _____   5. _____

3. _____

B. Write the spelling words that have the short *i* sound.

6. _____   9. _____

7. _____   10. _____

8. _____

C. Read each group of words. Circle the words that have the same vowel sound.

11. has   him   bad   14. has   six   will

12. fix   him   had   15. had   wag   will

13. six   sad   if

Name _____

has	rag	bad	six	kit
sat	had	pig	him	if

A. Write the spelling words that have the short *a* sound.

1. _____   4. _____

2. _____   5. _____

3. _____

B. Write the spelling words that have the short *i* sound.

6. _____   9. _____

7. _____   10. _____

8. _____

C. Read each group of words. Circle the words that have the same vowel sound.

11. pig   has   bad   14. sat   rag   him

12. kit   pig   rag   15. pig   sat   has

13. if   had   six

Name _____

| hasn't | snag | glad | slim | will |
| catch | hand | fixed | fits | if |

A. Write the spelling words that have the short *a* sound.

1. _____   4. _____

2. _____   5. _____

3. _____

B. Write the spelling words that have the short *i* sound.

6. _____   9. _____

7. _____   10. _____

8. _____

C. Read each group of words. Circle the words that have the same vowel sound.

11. will   hasn't   glad   14. slim   hand   catch

12. fixed   slim   snag   15. glad   will   if

13. if   glad   fits

Name _____

- A **sentence** is a group of words that tells a complete thought.
- Every sentence begins with a capital letter.
- A **statement** is a sentence that tells something.
- A statement ends with a period.

   Max is my friend.   He plays with me.

Circle the sentence in each row.

1. My friend helps me.   my friend helps me

2. Jake goes with me to the park   Jake goes with me to the park.

3. we walk to school together   We walk to school together.

4. Kara likes to dance.   Kara likes to dance

5. I showed Kara how to sing   I showed Kara how to sing.

6. I sing with my friend.   i sing with my friend.

Use the sentences as a model. Write about a time you played with a friend. Be sure to use complete sentences.

Name _____

> - A **question** is a sentence that asks something. It ends with a question mark.
> - A **statement** is a sentence that tells something. It ends with a period.
>
>   I play tag.   Will you play tag?

Read the sentences. Circle each question. Underline each statement.

1. Will Dad help you read the book?

2. Who are your friends?

3. I ate dinner at Lisa's house.

4. Sam helped me rake the leaves.

5. I watched Seth's game.

6. Will you go to the movies with me?

7. My friend takes care of me.

8. Sara shows Tad the new game.

9. Do you have homework tonight?

10. Friends help each other.

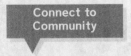 **Connect to Community** Write a list of questions about your community that you do not know the answers to.

Name _____

> • A "telling sentence," or **statement**, ends with a period.
> • An "asking sentence," or **question**, ends with a question mark.
>
>   Beth likes to laugh.   Do you like to laugh?

Read the sentences. Write the sentences correctly on the lines.

1. Donny sits next to me

_____

2. Will we have the same teacher

_____

3. The boys help Ben rake the leaves

_____

4. The friends walk to school

_____

5. Will you help me

_____

Name _____

- A **sentence** is a group of words that tells a complete thought.
- A "telling sentence," or **statement**, ends with a period.
- An "asking sentence," or **question**, ends with a question mark.

Read the passage. Discuss with a partner the difference between asking and telling. Circle each mistake in capitalization and punctuation. Then rewrite the passage correctly on the lines below.

    Jesse and Nico are friends Nico has to clean his room. Jesse will help him The boys work fast as a team? what will the boys do now. they will play baseball in Nico's yard

_____

_____

_____

_____

_____

Writing/Spelling Connection **Look through your notebook for statements and questions. Make sure you used periods and question marks correctly. Fix any mistakes.**

Name _____

Add the correct end mark to each sentence. Write S next to each statement. Write Q next to each question.

1. Ryan reads a book _____

2. He goes to the library _____

3. Who can go with him _____

4. His friend Hanna helps _____

5. Is it good to have a friend _____

6. Will Hanna help Ryan _____

7. How long have they been friends _____

8. What else do they do together _____

9. They play tag together _____

10. Does that sound like fun _____

Name _____

Expand your vocabulary by adding or removing inflectional endings, prefixes, or suffixes to a base word to create different forms of a word.

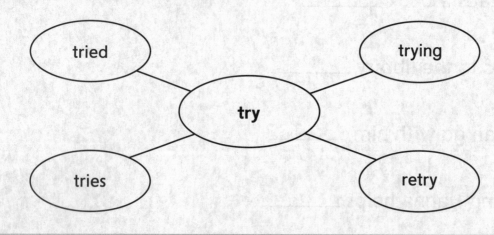

Use your notes from "Maria Celebrates Brazil." Choose one word and write it in the word web. Add circles to the web to write as many related words as you can. Use a dictionary to help you.

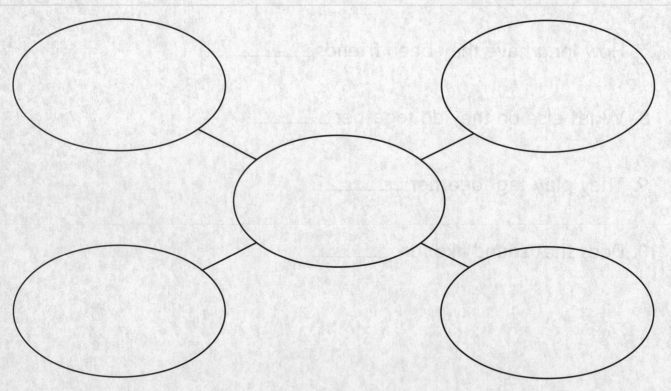

Name _____

Use a word from the box that matches the definition.

fair	plead	share	aside
language	culture	invited	scurries

1. The way we speak, read, or write _____

2. Treating others in a just and honest way _____

3. Goes or moves fast _____

4. To give part of something away _____

5. Out of the way _____

6. The way of life of a group of people at a certain time

   _____

7. To beg to get what you want _____

8. Asked someone to go somewhere or to do something

   _____

Name _____

Words that rhyme end with the same sounds.

Say each picture name. Then draw two pictures of things whose names rhyme with it.

1.		
2. 		
3.		
4.		

Teacher Directions: Read the box at the top of the page. Point to the pictures as you say *cat, hat, acrobat.* Emphasize the ending sounds in each word. Point out that all three words rhyme.

Name _____

Say each picture name. Circle the picture whose name has the same middle sound as the first picture in the row.

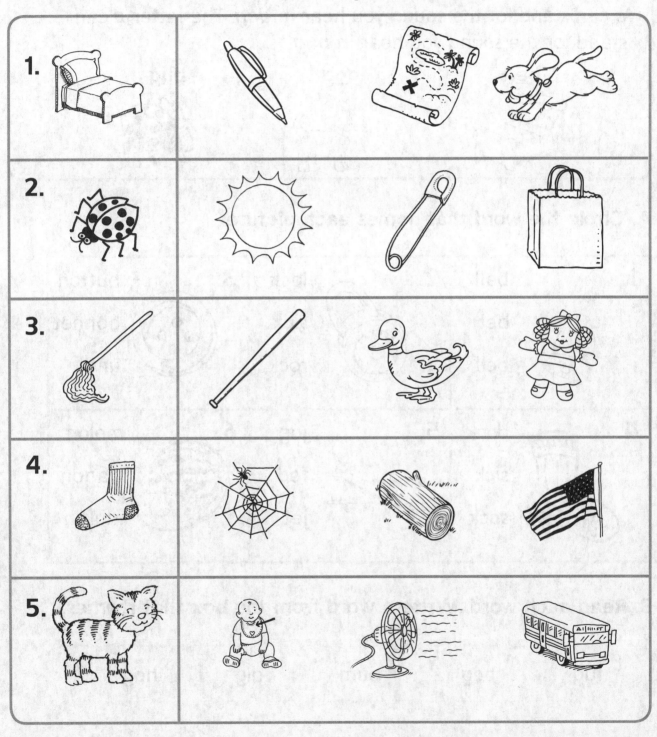

Teacher Directions: Model item 1. Say: /b/ /e/ /d/, stressing the vowel sound. Say *pen, map,* and *dog* and compare vowel sounds. Say: *The words* bed *and* pen *have the same middle sound:* /e/. Map *and* dog *have different middle sounds:* /a/ *and* /o/. Guide children to circle the picture of the pen.

Name _____

> The letter *e* can stand for the sound you hear in *bed.* The letter
> *o* can stand for the sound you hear in *dog.* The letter ***u*** can
> stand for the sound you hear in *bug.*
>
> **b<u>e</u>d**　　　　　**d<u>o</u>g**　　　　　**b<u>u</u>g**
>
> 　　　　

A. Circle the word that names each picture.

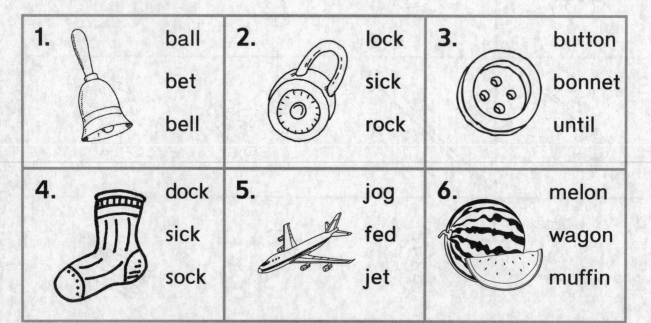

| 1. ball / bet / bell | 2. lock / sick / rock | 3. button / bonnet / until |
| 4. dock / sick / sock | 5. jog / fed / jet | 6. melon / wagon / muffin |

B. Read each word. Write a word from the box that rhymes.

> tug　　　　beg　　　　bum　　　　dig　　　　hog

1. fog _____　　2. egg _____

Name _____

A. Write *e, o,* or *u* to complete each picture name.

1. b _____ d

2.  r _____ g

3.  b _____ x

4. p _____ ppet

5.  j _____ t

6.  cobw_____ b

B. Change one letter at a time to make a new word with the short *e*, short *o*, or short *u* sound. The first one has been done for you. Finish the second ladder.

1. Go from **beg** to **pen**

2. Go from **bug** to **run**

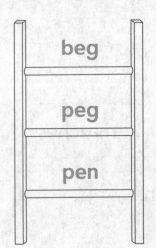

beg

peg

pen

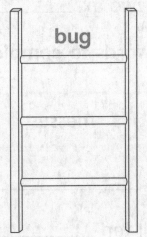

bug

Name _____

You can add the ending **-s** to a noun to name more than one.

When a noun ends in **-s, -ss, -sh, -ch,** or **-x**, add **-es** to tell about more than one.

rams   **glass_es_**   **fox_es_**

You can add **-s** or **-es** to a verb in the same way.

She sit_s_ on the chair.   **He fix_es_ his hair.**

A. Add -s or -es to the underlined word. Write the new word.

1. Ann <u>run</u> fast. _____

2. My dog <u>nap</u> in the sun. _____

3. Dad <u>rush</u> to work. _____

4. Tom had two <u>ax</u>. _____

B. Use the words to complete the sentences.

eggs   messes   mugs   matches

5. Mom put _____ in the pan.

6. He can fill ten _____ .

7. The pup gets in lots of _____ .

8. The team won both _____ .

Name _____

Read and spell the words in the box. Then identify which word completes the sentence.

could	find	funny	green	how
little	one	or	see	sounds

1. What you said was _____.

2. Do you want a blue hat _____
a red hat?

3. That van _____ loud.

4. There is only a _____ bit there.

5. The bug is _____ like the tree.

6. Do you _____ the map?

7. Dad could not _____ the lid for the box.

8. He has only _____ blue pen.

9. You _____ find my cat in there.

10. I see _____ to help Mom.

Teacher Directions: Point to the word *could*. Use the **Read/Spell/Write** routine. Repeat for each word in the box.

Name _____

Fold back the paper along the dotted line. Use the blanks to write each word as it is read aloud. When you finish the test, unfold the paper. Use the list at the right to correct any spelling mistakes.

1. _____ | **1.** went

2. _____ | **2.** tell

3. _____ | **3.** pet

4. _____ | **4.** job

5. _____ | **5.** fog

6. _____ | **6.** not

7. _____ | **7.** tug

8. _____ | **8.** hut

9. _____ | **9.** tub

10. _____ | **10.** bun

Review Words

11. _____ | **11.** fix

12. _____ | **12.** has

High-Frequency Words

13. _____ | **13.** one

14. _____ | **14.** or

15. _____ | **15.** see

Name _____

went	tell	pet	job	fog
not	tug	hut	tub	bun

A. Look at the spelling words in the box. Match each spelling word to a word below that has the same vowel sound. Write the words on the lines.

nut   *red*   *mop*

1. _____   5. _____   8. _____

2. _____   6. _____   9. _____

3. _____   7. _____   10. _____

4. _____

B. Read each group of words. Circle the words that have the same vowel sound.

11. not   job   went

12. tug   fog   bun

13. hut   tell   pet

14. bun   tell   tub

15. fog   not   hut

Name _____

net	leg	hog	job	bus
not	top	hut	tub	bun

A. Look at the spelling words in the box. Match each spelling word to a word below that has the same vowel sound.

nut

1. _____

2. _____

3. _____

4. _____

red

5. _____

6. _____

mop

7. _____

8. _____

9. _____

10. _____

B. Read each group of words. Circle the words that have the same vowel sound.

11. bun   leg   net

12. job   top   leg

13. bus   hog   tub

14. hut   bun   leg

15. hog   net   job

Name _____

| went | telling | peppy | sock | foggy |
| crops | tugged | fluffy | bathtub | muffin |

A. Look at the spelling words in the box. Match each spelling word to a word below that has the same vowel sound.

nut   *red*   *mop*

1. _____   5. _____   8. _____

2. _____   6. _____   9. _____

3. _____   7. _____   10. _____

4. _____

B. Read each group of words. Circle the words that have the same vowel sound.

11. bathtub   went   fluffy

12. crops   sock   peppy

13. muffin   foggy   tugged

14. tugged   went   telling

15. went   sock   foggy

Name _____

> • A **sentence** has a subject and an action word.
>
> • A **command** is a sentence that tells someone to do something.
>
> • A command ends with a period.
>
> • The subject of a command is the person to whom the speaker is talking.
>
>   Listen to your mother.   Play with your sister.

Underline each command.

1. My family eats dinner.

2. Set the table.

3. Use your napkin.

4. Grandma made tacos.

5. Give your sister the meat.

6. This tastes good.

 Use the sentences as a model. Write directions that explain how to complete a task. Be sure to use commands in your instructions.

Name _____

> • An **exclamation** is a sentence that shows strong feeling. It begins with a capital letter and ends with an exclamation point.
> • An **interjection** is a sudden remark. It begins with a capital letter and ends with an exclamation point.
>
> Maria can really dance!   Wow! Did you see her spin?

A. Circle each exclamation. Draw a line under each interjection.

1. Jane's family plays in the snow.

2. We can throw snowballs!

3. I want to make a snowman!

4. Oh, no! Dad lost his hat.

5. It's too cold outside!

6. Brrr! Let's sit by the fire.

B. Write a new exclamation or interjection on the line below.

7. _____

Connect to Community | **Explain ways to help the community when there is bad weather.**

Name _____

> • Begin each sentence with a capital letter.
> • End each **command** with a period.
> • End an **exclamation** with an exclamation point.
> • End an **interjection** with an exclamation point.
>   Get ready.   We can't be late!   Oh, no! We are late.

Read the sentences. Write the commands and exclamations correctly on the lines.

1. i can't wait for the Chinese festival

_____

2. come to the party with my family

_____

3. yummy nana's moon cakes are my favorite

_____

4. hey sit next to me

_____

5. Lee's dragon mask is cool

_____

6. hurray we love a parade

_____

Name _____

- Begin each sentence with a capital letter.
- An **exclamation** ends with an exclamation point.
- An **interjection** ends with an exclamation point.
- A **command** ends with a period.

Read the passage. Circle the mistakes in capitalization and punctuation. Then rewrite the passage correctly on the lines below.

let's visit Marco's house? his family is so much fun! shake his grandfather's hand. Say hello to him. I love his stories about Brazil. Hush. Let's listen?

_____

_____

_____

Look back through your notebook for commands, exclamations, and interjections you have used. Check that you used periods and exclamation points correctly. Fix any mistakes you find.

Name _____

Circle "command," "exclamation," or "interjection" for each sentence.

1. Have fun at the party.

   command   exclamation   interjection

2. It is Jen's birthday!

   command   exclamation   interjection

3. My family will surprise her!

   command   exclamation   interjection

4. Shhh! We can't tell Jen.

   command   exclamation   interjection

5. Come to my house at noon.

   command   exclamation   interjection

Rewrite the following sentences with correct capitalization and punctuation.

6. pick up another cake

   _____

7. Tad did a great job

   _____

Name _____

Look at this example of **context clues**. The underlined words explain what *polite* means.

He was **polite** because he knew <u>good manners were important</u>.

Read each sentence. Then circle the meaning of the word in bold print that makes sense. Underline the context clues.

1. "A snake will eat my bird!" **shrieked** Kim loudly.

   yelled   whispered

2. Jeff was **stumped** by his pet problem and didn't know how to solve it.

   made happy   confused

3. He wanted a pet that was different and **unique**.

   the same   not like others

4. What kind of pet wouldn't **disturb** or upset Kim?

   bother   enjoy

5. He was so **thrilled** to have a pet of his own that he shouted for joy.

   angry   excited

Name _____

> To figure out new words, look at word parts. A verb may have
> a base word plus the ending **-s, -es, -ed**, or **-ing**. The endings -s,
> -es, and -ing mean the action is happening now. The ending -ed
> means the action happened in the past.

Write the meaning of each underlined word. Circle whether the action is happening now or in the past.

1. "Will you help me fix my bike?" Squirrel <u>asked</u>.

   Meaning: _____

               now   past

2. "I'd like to help, but I am too busy <u>cooking</u> soup," said Fox.

   Meaning: _____

               now   past

3. "I'm too busy right now <u>washing</u> clothes."

   Meaning: _____

               now   past

4. Squirrel <u>explained</u> the problem.

   Meaning: _____

               now   past

5. Rabbit <u>looked</u> over the bike.

   Meaning: _____

               now   past

Name _____

Say the name of each picture. Say the middle sound. Circle the picture whose name has a different middle sound.

Teacher Directions: Model item 1. Say: *Listen to the middle sounds of these words:* pen, sun, mug. Stress the difference between short vowel sounds /e/ and /u/. Say: *I hear that the words* sun *and* mug *have the same middle sound: /u/. The word* pen *has the middle sound /e/.* Guide children to circle the picture of the pen.

Name _____

Listen to the word your teacher says. Change the sound. Circle the picture of the new word you made.

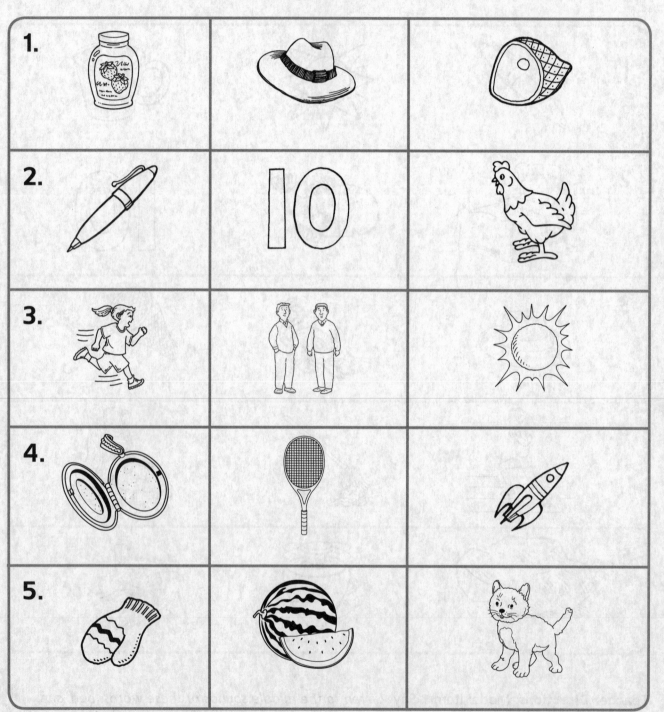

Teacher Directions: 1. Model: *This is the picture for the word* jam. *I can change the first sound /j/ to /h/ to make a new word. Listen to the new word:* ham. *I will circle the picture for the word* ham. **2.** Say *pen*. Change /p/ to /t/. **3.** Say *run*. Change /r/ to /s/. **4.** Say *locket*. Change /l/ to /r/. **5.** Say *mitten*. Change /m/ to /k/.

Name _____

Some words begin with a blend of sounds. Listen to the beginning sounds in the words **<u>cr</u>ab** and **<u>st</u>amp**. You can hear the sound for each letter in the blend.

<u>cr</u>ab   <u>st</u>amp

A. Look at each picture. Write the name of the picture on the line.

| step | clap | planet | trumpet | crack | grill |

1. _____   2. _____

3. _____   4. _____

5. _____   6. _____

B. Choose the word that completes each sentence. Then write the word on the line.

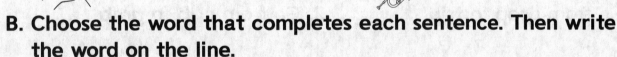

frog   track   blanket   stick

7. Tom threw the _____ to his dog.

8. Dan can run fast on the _____.

9. Ben says the best pet is a _____.

10. Do you have a warm _____?

Name _____

Some words begin with a blend of sounds. Listen to the beginning sounds in the words **_drip_** and **_grass_**. You can hear the sound for each letter in the blend.

d̲rip   g̲rass

A. Write the missing letters to finish the picture name.

 1. 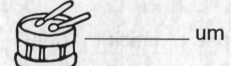 _____ um

2.  _____ ossom

 3. _____ uck

4.  _____ icket

B. Change one letter at a time to make a new word. The first one has been done for you. Finish the second ladder.

1. Go from **drop** to **trip**.

2. Go from **crib** to **grab**

drop

drip

trip

crib

Name _____

A **closed syllable** ends with a consonant. It has a short vowel sound. Some words have two closed syllables. Read the word *sunset*. You can see that each syllable ends with a consonant.

su<u>n</u>se<u>t</u>

A. Put the two closed syllables together to form a word that matches the picture. Then write and read the word.

1. pen   cil   _____

2. pup   pet   _____

3. mit   ten   _____

4. den   tist   _____

B. Complete each sentence using a word from above.

5. This _____ is a lion.

6. The _____ fixes my teeth.

Name _____

Read and spell the words in the box. Then identify which word completes the sentence.

boy	by	girl	he	hear
she	small	want	were	what

1. I _____ a blue pen.

2. She did not _____ me say so.

3. They _____ both a lot of help to me.

4. That boy seems like _____ cannot find his ball.

5. I know _____ we can do.

6. That girl said _____ and her sister could help.

7. The red ball is _____ the rock there.

8. You had one like that when you were _____ .

9. When she was a _____, she had a yellow cat.

10. This hat was his when he was a little _____ .

Teacher Directions: Point to the word *boy*. Use the **Read/Spell/Write** routine. Repeat for each word in the box.

Name _____

Fold back the paper along the dotted line. Use the blanks to write each word as it is read aloud. When you finish the test, unfold the paper. Use the list at the right to correct any spelling mistakes.

1. _____

2. _____

3. _____

4. _____

5. _____

6. _____

7. _____

8. _____

9. _____

10. _____

Review Words 11. _____

12. _____

High-Frequency Words 13. _____

14. _____

15. _____

1. grass

2. trips

3. crack

4. still

5. west

6. mask

7. clap

8. plans

9. milk

10. belt

11. fog

12. tub

13. by

14. he

15. she

Name _____

> | grass | trips | crack | still | west |
> |-------|-------|-------|-------|------|
> | mask | clap | plans | milk | belt |

A. Look at the spelling words in the box. Write words in the column with the correct two-letter blend.

r-blends: *cr, tr, gr*	*s*-blends: *st, sk*	*l*-blends: *cl, pl, lk, lt*
1. _____	4. _____	7. _____
2. _____	5. _____	8. _____
3. _____	6. _____	9. _____
		10. _____

B. Write the spelling word that has the same pattern as each word below.

11. risk _____

12. trots _____

13. plops _____

14. list _____

15. tilt _____

Name _____

plan	crack	stop	nest	grass
milk	mask	trip	clap	belt

A. Look at the spelling words in the box. Write words in the column with the correct two-letter blend.

r-blends: cr, tr, gr	*s*-blends: st, sk	*l*-blends: cl, pl, lk, lt
1. _____	4. _____	7. _____
2. _____	5. _____	8. _____
3. _____	6. _____	9. _____
		10. _____

B. Write the spelling word that has the same pattern as each word below.

11. play _____

12. list _____

13. felt _____

14. green _____

15. sulk _____

Name _____

cracks	mask	planning	belt	grass
clapped	trips	west	milk	still

A. Look at the spelling words in the box. Write words in the column with the correct two-letter blend.

r-blends: *cr, tr, gr*	*s*-blends: *st, sk*	*l*-blends: *cl, pl, lk, lt*
1. _____	4. _____	7. _____
2. _____	5. _____	8. _____
3. _____	6. _____	9. _____
		10. _____

B. Write a spelling word that has the same pattern as each word below.

11. played _____

12. steal _____

13. adult _____

14. grant _____

15. silk _____

Name _____

> • A **subject** tells who or what the sentence is about.
> • The **subject** is often at the beginning of a sentence.
>
> <u>The cat</u> is white.   <u>Jim and Pam</u> like cats.

A. Underline the subject in each sentence.

1. Sam has a pet dog.

2. His dog can run fast after a ball.

3. Sam and his dog have a ball that is red.

4. Mom and Dad will pet the dog.

B. Write two more sentences about pets. Underline each subject.

_____

_____

_____

_____

 Use the sentences as a model. Write about a pet that you have or wish you had. Be sure to use complete sentences including subjects and predicates.

Name _____

- A **subject** tells who or what the sentence is about.
- A group of words without a subject or predicate is not a complete sentence.
- An incomplete sentence is a **fragment**.

  Fragment: Cal

  Fragment: owns a bunny.

  Complete sentence: Cal owns a bunny.

Complete each sentence by adding a subject.

1. _____ has a pet cat.

2. _____ both like little pets.

3. _____ gets a green ball for her pet dog.

4. _____ runs fast and jumps.

5. _____ want a pet like that.

6. _____ will find a big yellow ball for his pet.

Connect to Community   Explain ways to help animals in need in your community.

Name _____

> • Use **quotation marks** at the beginning and at the end
>   of the exact words a person says.
> • The punctuation at the end of the speaker's words is
>   also included inside the quotation marks.
>
>   "Why don't you help Dad?" Mom asked.
>
>   "I like to help," Sarah said.

**Write each sentence. Add quotation
marks where they are needed.**

1. I am making some cookies, Dad said.

_____

2. I want to help you, Sarah said.

_____

3. Dad said, Your job can be to get me the butter.

_____

4. Sarah asked, What else can I do to help?

_____

5. You can help me eat the cookies, Dad said.

_____

Name _____

> • The **subject** of a sentence is who or what the sentence is about.
> • Every sentence has a subject, and the subject agrees with the verb.

A. Draw a line below each subject in the paragraph.

Ann has a kitten. The kitten is little. Ann pets the kitten. She lets her friends pet the kitten, too. The kitten is happy. The kitten runs and jumps. Ann calls the kitten Tom. Tom is glad to be Ann's kitten. Tom sits on Ann's lap and lets Ann pet him. Ann's dad and mom are glad to see them both so happy. They pet Tom and get him a cat tree.

B. Write a subject on the line to complete each sentence.

1. _____ has a kitten.

2. _____ is little.

3. _____ is called Tom.

4. _____ runs and jumps.

5. _____ pets Tom.

6. _____ sits on Ann's lap.

7. _____ are both happy.

8. _____ can all pet the kitten, too.

9. _____ are glad to see Ann and Tom so happy.

10. _____ get a cat tree for Tom.

Name _____

Circle the correct answer.

1. Circle the answer that has the subject underlined correctly.

   A. Jill has a pet <u>frog</u>.　　B. Jill has a <u>pet</u> frog.

   C. Jill <u>has</u> a pet frog.　　D. <u>Jill</u> has a pet frog.

2. Circle the answer that shows a complete sentence.

   A. My pet is.　　　　　B. My pet is a cat.

   C. A cat.　　　　　　　D. Is a cat.

3. What word is the subject of this sentence?

   Cats can run fast.

   A. Cats　　　　　　　B. can

   C. run　　　　　　　　D. fast

4. What is the subject of this sentence?

   The dog runs to get the red ball.

   A. the red ball　　　　B. to get

   C. runs　　　　　　　　D. The dog

Writing/Spelling Connection

Look back through your notebook for verbs you have used. Make sure they agree with their subjects. Fix any mistakes you find.

Name _____

Expand your vocabulary by adding or removing inflectional endings, prefixes, or suffixes to a base word to create different forms of a word.

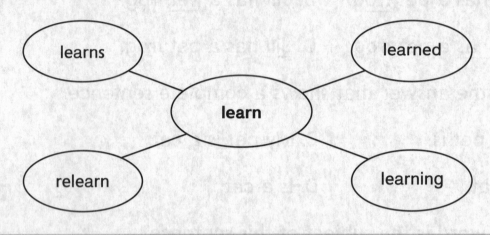

Use your notes from "Little Flap Learns to Fly." Choose one word and write it in the word web. Add circles to the web to write as many related words as you can. Use a dictionary to help you.

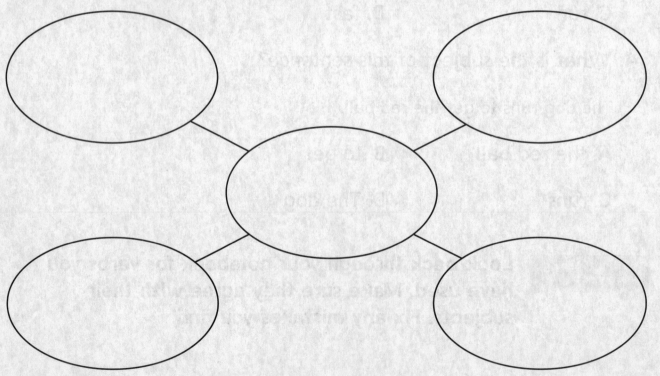

Name _____

Draw lines to match the words with their meanings.

1. depends

2. share

3. invited

4. rescue

5. culture

6. plead

7. nervously

8. afraid

A. The way of life of a group of people

B. To give away part of something

C. Feeling fear

D. Asked someone to go somewhere or do something

E. Relies on or trusts

F. To save from danger or harm

G. To beg or ask seriously for something

H. Showing worry about what could happen

Name _____

Say the picture name. Then say the sounds in the word, one at a time. Draw an X in the box for each sound you hear. Write the number of sounds on the line.

1.   _____

2.  _____

3.  _____

4.   _____

5.   _____

Teacher Directions: Model 1. *I can say the sounds in the word* gate. *The word* gate *has three sounds: /g/ /ā/ /t/. Say the sounds with me.* Guide children to draw 3 X's and write the amount of sounds for #1.

Name _____

Say the name of each picture. Say the middle sound. Circle the picture whose name has a different middle sound.

Teacher Directions: Model item 1. Say: *Listen to the middle sounds of these words:* cake, rake, map. Stress the difference between vowel sounds /ā/ and /a/. Say: *I hear that the words* cake *and* rake *have the same middle sound:* /ā/. *The word* map *has the middle sound* /a/. Guide children to circle the picture of the map.

Name _____

The long *a* sound you hear in **cake** can be spelled with ***a_e***.

c<u>a</u>k<u>e</u>

A. Read the words in the box. Circle the words that have the long *a* sound.

parade	plane	glass	rake
cape	stand	cupcake	back

B. Use a word from the box above to name each picture below. Write each word on the line.

1.  _____

2.  _____

3.  _____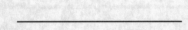

4.  _____

5.  _____

Name _____

> The letter ***a*** can stand for the short ***a*** sound you hear in ***can***.
> The long ***a*** sound you hear in ***cane*** can be spelled with ***a_e.***
>
> c<u>a</u>n   c<u>a</u>n<u>e</u>
>
>

A. Write the correct letters to complete each picture name.

1.  f _____   2.   m _____

3.  gr _____   4.   j _____

5.  par _____   6.    panc _____

B. Change one letter at a time to make a new word with the short *a* or Long *a*: *a_e* sound.

7. Go from **pan** to **tap**   8. Go from **mane** to **fake**

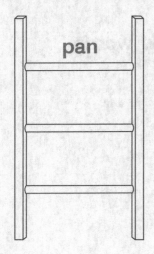

Name _____

> The ending **-ed** can be added to an action word to show that an action has already happened.
>
> **pack**   **pack<u>ed</u>**
>
> The **-ing** ending in an action word means that the action is happening now.
>
> **smell**   **smell<u>ing</u>**

A. Circle the word that completes each sentence. Then write the word.

1. Dad _____ the lamp.

   fixed   fixing

2. Jeff is _____ Mrs. Lin for help.

   asked   asking

3. Pat is _____ on nuts.

   snacked   snacking

4. My dog _____ up on my lap.

   jumped   jumping

5. Dad is _____ his red truck.

   washed   washing

B. Add -ed and -ing to each word to make new words. Write the words on the lines below.

6. rest _____ _____

7. look _____ _____

8. start _____ _____

Name _____

Read and spell the words in the box. Then identify which word completes the sentence.

another	done	into	move	now
show	too	water	year	your

1. I put _____ in the tub.

2. Do you want to go _____?

3. Tim bumped _____ the desk.

4. What trips did you go on this _____?

5. _____ me how to do this.

6. Can I see _____ green hat?

7. I want _____ glass of water.

8. My family will _____ to a new place next year.

9. When will you be _____ cooking dinner?

10. Thomas is going to camp this summer, _____.

Teacher Directions: Point to the word *another.* Use the **Read/Spell/Write** routine. Repeat for each word in the box.

Name _____

Fold back the paper along the dotted line. Use the blanks to write each word as it is read aloud. When you finish the test, unfold the paper. Use the list at the right to correct any spelling mistakes.

1. _____   1. bag

2. _____   2. cap

3. _____   3. ham

4. _____   4. bake

5. _____   5. ate

6. _____   6. mad

7. _____   7. back

8. _____   8. cape

9. _____   9. made

10. _____   10. rake

Review Words   11. _____   11. still

12. _____   12. belt

High-Frequency Words   13. _____   13. into

14. _____   14. done

15. _____   15. your

Name _____

| bag | cap | ham | bake | ate |
| mad | back | cape | made | rake |

A. Write the spelling words that have the short *a* sound as in *plan*.

1. _____ 3. _____ 5. _____

2. _____ 4. _____

B. Write the spelling words that have the long *a* sound as in *plane*.

6. _____ 8. _____ 10. _____

7. _____ 9. _____

C. Read each group of words. Circle the words that have the same vowel sound.

11. bag   cap   bake   14. bake   back   bag

12. cap   rake   cape   15. ate   mad   made

13. ham   ate   mad

Name _____

```
bag        tap        ham        bake       ate
mad        tan        pal        made       late
```

A. Write the spelling words that have the short *a* sound as in *plan*.

1. _____   4. _____

2. _____   5. _____

3. _____   6. _____

B. Write the spelling words that have the long *a* sound as in *plane*.

7. _____   9. _____

8. _____   10. _____

C. Read each group of words. Circle the words that have the same vowel sound.

11. ham   tap   ate   14. late   pal   ham

12. late   bag   bake   15. bag   made   late

13. mad   tan   made

Name _____

safety	flames	male	vat	ate
clapping	back	cape	making	rake

A. Write the spelling words that have the short *a* sound as in *plan*.

1. _____   3. _____

2. _____

B. Write the spelling words that have the long *a* sound as in *plane*.

4. _____   8. _____

5. _____   9. _____

6. _____   10. _____

7. _____

C. Read each group of words. Circle the words that have the same vowel sound.

11. safety   back   cape   **14.** vat   safety   making

12. vat   making   back   **15.** back   clapping   ate

13. flames   rake   clapping

Name _____

> • Every sentence has a subject and a predicate.
> • The **subject** tells who or what the sentence is about.
> • A **predicate** tells what the subject does or is.
>   Les <u>has a dog</u>.

A. Draw a line from each subject on the left to its predicate on the right.

1. The cat   runs to get the ball.

2. Dad and Mom   pets the dog.

3. The dog   runs up a tree.

4. Bill   get the cat from the tree.

B. Draw a circle around the predicate.

5. The girl and boy go there every day.

6. The little boy has a yellow hat.

7. They both have small boxes.

 Use the sentences as a model. Write about an interaction you have had with a pet or animal. Notice the importance of nouns when writing your sentences.

Name _____

> - A **predicate** tells what the subject of a sentence does or is.
> - A predicate is often at the end of a sentence.
> - A group of words without a predicate is an incomplete sentence, or a sentence **fragment.**
> - You can correct a sentence fragment by adding a predicate.
>
> Fragment: Liz
>
> Complete sentence: Liz has a big blue box.

Circle the predicate that completes each sentence.

1. Liz _____.

A. her box.   B. opens her box.

2. The box _____.

A. has a blue hat in it.   B. blue hat.

3. Sten _____.

A. and Liz.   B. has a yellow box.

4. He _____.

A. yellow hat.   B. finds a yellow hat in it.

Connect to Community **Explain ways to help animals in your community.**

Name _____

> • Use **quotation marks** at the beginning and at the end of the exact words a person says.
> • The punctuation at the end of the speaker's words is also included inside the quotation marks.
>
> > "How are you?" Mom asked.
> >
> > "I am sad," Billy said.

Write each sentence. Add quotation marks where they are needed.

1. Mom asked, Why are you sad?

_____

2. I have lost my red ball, Billy said. I cannot find it at all.

_____

3. Mom asked, Is that your red ball next to the big rock?

_____

4. Thank you, Mom! said Billy. That is my red ball right there!

_____

5. You are welcome, Mom said.

_____

Name _____

> • A **predicate** tells what the subject of a sentence does or is.
>
> • A predicate is often at the end of a sentence.
>
> • A group of words without a predicate is an incomplete sentence, or a sentence **fragment**.

A. Read the passage. Underline the predicates.

Nella sees a big bag on the table. She wants to see what is in the bag. But she is not tall. She cannot see. Nella's dad gets the bag. He puts it where Nella can see in it. The bag has a doll in it! The doll has a blue dress and a blue hat. It is an old doll.

B. Write a predicate to correct each fragment with words that Nella's dad says to her.

1. This doll _____

_____

2. Your Grandma _____

_____

3. You _____

_____

4. This doll _____

Writing/Spelling Connection

Look back through your notebook and notice the subjects and predicates you have used. Make sure each of your sentences has a subject and a predicate.

Name _____

A. Underline the predicate in each sentence.

1. The pond has ducks in it.

2. The ducks swim in the pond.

3. The tall trees are by the pond.

4. The trees are nut trees.

5. They make nuts we can eat.

6. Ducks do not eat nuts.

7. Dad says the nuts are too big for ducks.

8. The ducks can eat small seeds and grass.

9. Ducks can eat bugs, too.

10. I would not want to eat what ducks eat!

B. Write a predicate to complete each sentence.

11. One duck _____

_____

12. The trees by the pond _____

_____

13. The nuts from the trees _____

_____

Name _____

> To figure out a new word, look for a **prefix**, or word part at the beginning of the word.
>
> The prefix *re-* means "again."
>
> The prefix *un-* means "not."
>
> The prefix *dis-* means "opposite of."

Read each sentence. Underline the word that has a prefix. Then write the word and its meaning.

1. The others disagree.

_____

2. They look up but are unable to see anything.

_____

3. Its brown color makes it seem to disappear into the trees.

_____

4. The deer slips away unseen.

_____

5. The class retraces their steps back to the bus.

_____

Name _____

> To figure out a new word, separate the **base word** from the ending. When added to verbs, the endings *-s, -es,* and *-ing* mean the action is happening now. The ending *-ed* means the action happened in the past.

A. Read each sentence. Look at each underlined word. Draw a line between the base word and the ending.

1. Van's eyes <u>opened</u> wide.

2. Food booths were set up <u>showing</u> colorful flags.

3. People were <u>selling</u> Greek salad there.

B. Underline the verb in each sentence. Then change each verb so that it tells about an action happening now. Write the new word.

4. Mom stopped at the first booth.

   _____

5. At last, the family reached the end of the street.

   _____

Name _____

Say each picture name. Say the middle sound. Circle the picture with the same middle sound as the first picture in the row.

Teacher Directions: Model item 1 by saying *top, grapes, clock,* and *bell.* Repeat, stressing the vowel sounds. Say: *The words* top *and* clock *have the same middle sound: /o/.* Grapes *and* bell *have different middle sounds: /ā/ and /e/.* Guide children to circle the picture of the clock.

Name _____

Say the name of the first picture. Circle the picture in the same row that has the same middle sound as the first picture.

Teacher Directions: 1. Model: *Listen to the middle sounds of these words:* bib, wig, ham. Stress the difference between short vowel sounds /i/ and /a/. *I hear that the word* wig *has the same middle sound, /i/, as* bib. *The word* ham *has the middle sound /a/.* Guide children to circle the picture of the wig.

Name _____

> The letter *i* can stand for the sound you hear in the middle of *wig*. It can also stand for the sound you hear in the middle of *nine*.

 w<u>i</u>g

nine

A. Circle the word that names each picture.

1. bit / bike / hike	2. pine / pin / pan	3. line / like / lip
4. dim / mad / dime	5. behave / beehive / beside	6. combine / capsize / cabin

B. Write a word that names each picture.

7. 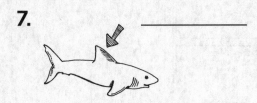 _____

8. 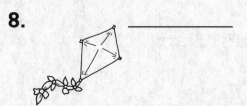 _____

Name _____

A. Circle the word to complete the sentence. Write the word.

1. Mom can run a _____.

mile   mill

2. I will take a little _____ of water.

bit   bite

3. Dave said this lime is not _____.

rip   ripe

4. We had a _____ lunch in the park.

picnic   panic

5. A snake is a kind of _____.

retire   reptile

6. I like to play on the _____.

slid   slide

B. Finish each word ladder. Change one letter at a time.

7. Go from **hike** to **tide**.   8. Go from **nine** to **pipe**.

Name _____

> A **possessive noun** ends with an apostrophe (') and an *s* to show who owns something, such as *Meg's bike.*

Rewrite each phrase using a possessive noun.

1. the snack that belongs to the boy _____

2. the tent that belongs to Dad _____

3. the skates that belong to Mom _____

4. the smile that belongs to Dave _____

5. the string that belongs to the kite _____

6. the hand that belongs to Jill _____

7. the cup that belongs to the girl _____

8. the nap that belongs to the cat _____

9. the pond that belongs to the frog _____

10. the socks that belong to Jan _____

Name _____

Read and spell the words in the box. Then identify which word completes the sentence.

all	any	goes	new	number
other	right	says	understands	work

1. My dad _____ what I like.

2. _____ of the boxes are filled.

3. My mom and dad _____ there.

4. His left sock did not go with his _____ sock.

5. The band played a _____ song.

6. Do you have _____ grapes for me?

7. He _____ that they have snacks.

8. She _____ there to see her sister.

9. We can take the _____ path.

10. He came in on track _____ nine.

Teacher Directions: Point to the word *all*. Use the **Read/Spell/Write** routine. Repeat for each word in the box.

Name _____

Fold back the paper along the dotted line. Use the blanks to write each word as it is read aloud. When you finish the test, unfold the paper. Use the list at the right to correct any spelling mistakes.

1. _____
2. _____
3. _____
4. _____
5. _____
6. _____
7. _____
8. _____
9. _____
10. _____

Review Words

11. _____
12. _____

High-Frequency Words

13. _____
14. _____
15. _____

1. did
2. fin
3. pick
4. line
5. pipe
6. tip
7. mix
8. five
9. side
10. hike
11. cape
12. made
13. all
14. any
15. says

Name _____

did	fin	pick	line	pipe
tip	mix	five	side	hike

A. Write the spelling words that have the short *i* sound spelled *i* as in *big*.

1. _____   3. _____   5. _____

2. _____   4. _____

B. Write the spelling words that have the long *i* sound spelled *i_e* as in *time*.

6. _____   8. _____   10. _____

7. _____   9. _____

C. Write a spelling word that rhymes with each word below.

11. bike _____   16. ride _____

12. hid _____   17. ripe _____

13. fine _____   18. dive _____

14. lick _____

15. fix _____

Name _____

did	kite	win	line	pipe
tip	mix	five	hit	hive

A. Write the spelling words that have the short _i_ sound.

1. _____   4. _____

2. _____   5. _____

3. _____

B. Write the spelling words that have the long _i_ sound.

6. _____   9. _____

7. _____   10. _____

8. _____

C. Write a spelling word that rhymes with each word below.

11. bite _____   15. fix _____

12. hid _____   16. pin _____

13. fine _____   17. ripe _____

14. lip _____   18. bit _____

Name _____

hive	finish	picked	line	times
rips	smiling	bricks	sideways	hiked

A. Write the spelling words that have the short *i* sound.

1. _____   3. _____

2. _____   4. _____

B. Write the spelling words that have the long *i* sound.

5. _____   8. _____

6. _____   9. _____

7. _____   10. _____

C. Write a spelling word that rhymes with each word below.

11. lips _____   15. dive _____

12. fine _____   16. liked _____

13. licked _____   17. piling _____

14. fix _____   18. limes _____

Name _____

> • When you **expand a sentence**, you add simple **modifiers**, or details, to the subject or predicate.
>
> The boy helps. The young boy helps.
>
> The man rakes. The man rakes leaves.

A. Add simple modifiers to the subjects of these sentences.

Write the new sentences on the lines.

1. The boys worked in the garden.

_____

2. The gardener gave them some seeds.

_____

3. The seeds were in bags.

_____

B. Add simple modifiers to the predicates of these sentences.

Write the new sentences on the lines.

4. The boys planted.

_____

5. The gardener smiled.

_____

Name _____

> • When two sentences have the same subject, you can use the word **and** to combine the predicates.
>
> Anna swept the floor.　　　　　Anna fed the cat.
>
> Anna swept the floor <u>and</u> fed the cat.
>
> • When two sentences have the same predicate, you can use the word **and** to combine the subjects.
>
> Anna liked to help.　　　　　Terry liked to help.
>
> Anna <u>and</u> Terry liked to help.

Use *and* to combine each pair of sentences. Write the new sentence.

1. Petra cleaned the kitchen.
Randy cleaned the kitchen.

_____

2. Jen fed the cat.　　　　　Jen fed the dog.

_____

3. Jim swept the steps.　　　　　Jim washed the car.

_____

 Use the sentences as a model. Write about a time you have helped someone work outside. Include more details than you normally would to expand your sentences.

Name _____

- A **series** is a set of three or more words.
- Use commas to separate three or more words in a series.
- The word **and** or **or** comes before the last word in a series.
    Ducks eat <u>fish</u>, <u>plants</u>, and <u>insects</u>.
    Ducks can be <u>white</u>, <u>black</u>, or <u>brown</u>.

A. Write the correct sentence on the line.

1. Ducks swim walk and fly.

_____

2. They quack when they are hungry mad or surprised.

_____

B. Write two sentences that each contain a series. Be sure to add the commas in each series.

3. _____

4. _____

Connect to Community Explain how you and your friends or siblings can help your community. Practice combining sentences.

Name _____

- When you **expand a sentence**, you add more details to the subject or predicate.
- When two sentences have the same subject, you can use the word **and** to combine the predicates.
- When two sentences have the same predicate, you can use the word **and** to combine the subjects.

Read the paragraphs. Combine sentences where possible. Then rewrite correctly on the lines.

Ben made a cake. Ben put frosting on it. Ben's dad saw the cake. Ben's sister saw the cake. They both wanted some of it.

Ben saw them. Ben said, "That cake is for my club, not for you." Ben's dad felt sad. Ben's sister felt sad.

Ben said, "But I am making another cake. The next cake is even better. The next cake is all for you!"

_____

_____

_____

_____

_____

_____

Name _____

Circle the parts of the sentences that can be combined with the word *and*. Combine the sentences. Write the new sentence on the line.

1. Paul's father went to fight the fire.
   Paul's uncle went to fight the fire.

   _____

2. Paul visited the fire station.
   Ellen visited the fire station.

   _____

3. Firefighters work in the daytime.
   Firefighters work at night.

   _____

4. They clean the hoses.
   They clean the fire trucks.

   _____

5. Ellen asked questions.
   Ellen listened to the answers.

   _____

6. Paul listened.
   Paul learned a lot.

   _____

Name _____

Synonyms are words that have almost the same meaning.
For example, the words *small and tiny* are synonyms.

A. Read the sentences. Write a word to answer each question.

Your family's new dinner plates are so pretty!
The dishes at my house are not as beautiful as these.

1. Which word in the second sentence is a synonym for **plates**?

    _____

2. Which word in the second sentence is a synonym for **pretty**?

    _____

B. Write two different synonyms for the word in ( ) to complete each sentence.

3. (big) The mountains are _____, and the trees are
   _____.

4. (good) My friends are _____, and we have
   _____ times together.

5. (said) I _____ his name, and he _____
   my name.

Name _____

Read the clues. Complete the puzzle with your vocabulary words. Use the letters in the boxes to solve the riddle.

actions	aside	peered	language
perfectly	secret	nervously	scurries

1. Out of the way ▢ _ _ _ _

2. Known to few ▢ _ _ _ _ _

3. Without fault ▢ _ _ _ _ _ _ _ _

4. Goes or moves in a hurry _ _ _ _ _ _ _ _

5. Showing worry about what could happen _ _ _ _ ▢ _ _ _ _

6. Things done or performed _ _ _ _ _ ▢ _

7. Spoken or written words _ _ _ _ _ _ ▢ _

8. Looked hard or tried to see something _ _ _ _ ▢ _

What is full of holes but can still hold water?

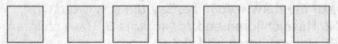

Name _____

Listen to each word your teacher says. Add the beginning sound. Circle the picture of the new word you made.

1.

2.

3.

4.

5.

  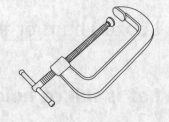

Teacher Directions: 1. Model: *I can add sounds to words to make new words. Listen to the word:* ice. *I can add /m/ to the beginning of* ice *to make the new word* mice. *Say the new word with me:* mice. *Then circle the picture that shows it.* **2.** Have children add /p/ to *ants*. **3.** Have children add /s/ to *top*. **4.** Have children add /p/ to *up*. **5.** Have children add /k/ to *lamp*.

Name _____

Listen to the sounds your teacher says. Blend the sounds to make a word. Circle the picture that goes with that word.

1.

2.

3.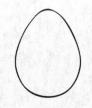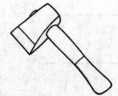

4.

5.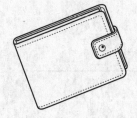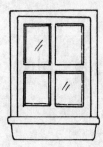

Teacher Directions: Model item 1 by saying: */h/ /ā/. Listen as I blend these sounds: /hāāā/,* hay. *I see a picture that shows hay, so I will circle it.* Guide children to blend the sounds and circle the picture. For items 2-5, have children listen to the sounds, blend them to form a word, and circle the correct picture. **2.** Say: /t/ /ō/; **3.** Say: /e/ /g/; **4.** Say: /s/ /t/ /a/ /m/ /p/; **5.** Say: /w/ /i/ /n/ /d/ /ō/.

Name _____

The long *o* sound you hear in **cone** can be spelled with **o_e**.

c<u>o</u>n<u>e</u>

A. Use a word from the box to complete each sentence.

bone	on	topic	alone

1. The cat sits _____ top of the mat.

2. The dog ate the _____.

3. I walked home _____.

4. What is the _____ of the book?

B. Circle the word with the short *o* sound. Then write the word.

5. ox bone _____

6. globe blocks _____

7. hose box _____

Name_____

> The letter *o* can stand for the short *o* sound you hear in *cot*.
>
> c<u>o</u>t

A. Look at each picture. Read the words and circle the one that names the picture. Write the word.

1.

_____

robe   rob   rub

2.

_____

con   cone   clap

3.

_____

lot   glob   globe

4.

_____

note   nut   not

5.

_____

topic   poles   tadpole

6.

_____

lock   lemon   locket

B. Go back and underline the letters that stand for the long *o* sound in the answers above. Circle the letters that stand for the short *o* sound in the answers above.

Name _____

> The *-ing* ending in an action word means that the action is happening now. The *-ed* ending means that the action happened in the past.
>
> **smelling**    **kicked**

Read the sentences and words. Circle the word that completes each sentence. Then write the word.

1. Dad _____ the lamp.

        fix   fixed

2. Ken is _____ Ben in class.

        help   helping

3. My dog _____ up on my lap.

        jumped   jump

4. Pam _____ her milk.

        spill   spilled

5. Dad is _____ his red truck.

        wash   washing

Name _____

Complete each sentence. Use the words in the box.

because	cold	family	friends	have
know	off	picture	school	took

1. My sister Jen is part of my _____.

2. I _____ the math facts.

3. Turn the light _____ when you go.

4. The _____ is hanging on the wall.

5. The _____ wind moves the trees.

6. He _____ the gum and thanked her.

7. Do you _____ a pen?

8. Our _____ moved next door.

9. The _____ is closed today.

10. We play together _____ we are friends.

Name _____

Fold back the paper along the dotted line. Use the blanks to write each word as it is read aloud. When you finish the test, unfold the paper. Use the list at the right to correct any spelling mistakes.

1. _____
2. _____
3. _____
4. _____
5. _____
6. _____
7. _____
8. _____
9. _____
10. _____

Review Words

11. _____
12. _____

High-Frequency Words

13. _____
14. _____
15. _____

1. box
2. fox
3. dog
4. lock
5. pot
6. cone
7. home
8. nose
9. poke
10. rope
11. side
12. line
13. have
14. off
15. took

Name _____

box	fox	dog	lock	pot
cone	home	nose	poke	rope

A. Write the spelling words that have the short *o* sound as in *on*.

1. _____   2. _____   3. _____

4. _____   5. _____

B. Write the spelling words that have the long *o* sound as in *note*.

6. _____   7. _____   8. _____

9. _____   10. _____

C. Read each group of words. Circle the words that have the same vowel sound.

11. box   dog   home

12. poke   fox   nose

13. rope   lock   cone

14. pot   poke   lock

15. cone   lock   box

Name _____

---

box	fox	dog	bone	pot
home	hope	nose	long	rope

A. Write the spelling word that has the short *o* sound as in *on*.

1. _____   4. _____

2. _____   5. _____

3. _____

B. Write the spelling words that have the long *o* sound as in *note*.

6. _____   9. _____

7. _____   10. _____

8. _____

C. Read each group of words. Circle the words that have the same vowel sound.

11. fox   long   bone   14. home fox   box

12. pot   nose   home   15. pot   home rope

13. bone   dog   hope

Name _____

stove	foxes	notebook	locked	plot
close	wrote	smoke	poked	phone

A. Write the spelling word that has the short _o_ sound as in _on_.

1. _____   3. _____

2. _____

B. Write the spelling words that have the long _o_ sound as in _note_.

4. _____   8. _____

5. _____   9. _____

6. _____   10. _____

7. _____

C. Read each group of words. Circle the words that have the same vowel sound.

11. close   plot   wrote   14. plot   phone   locked

12. foxes   poked plot   15. locked   notebook phone

13. smoke   stove   foxes

Name _____

> • A **noun** is a word that names something.
> • Some nouns name people.
>   Our <u>teacher</u> has a cat.

A. Circle the nouns that name people in each sentence.

1. The boy walks his dog.

2. His mother takes the bag.

3. My sister sees a frog.

4. The family visits the park.

5. A farmer plants her seeds.

6. A baby smiles at the cat.

B. Write two sentences about people. Circle each noun that names a person.

7. _____

_____

8. _____

_____

 Use the sentences as a model. Write about an interaction you have had with a pet or animal. Notice the importance of nouns when writing your sentences.

Name _____

- A **noun** is a word that names a person, a place, or a thing.
- Some nouns name a person.
  My <u>teacher</u> hands us pencils.
- Some nouns name a place. • Some nouns name a thing.
  The <u>beach</u> is fun.   <u>Snow</u> is cold.

A. Circle the nouns. Then underline the nouns that name a place or a thing.

1. Her grandmother lives in the desert.

2. My father showed me a lizard.

3. My sister puts food in a dish.

4. His grandfather hiked up the path.

5. Our teacher read about penguins.

B. Write a sentence about a place or a thing. Circle the nouns in the sentence.

6. _____

_____

Explain ways to help the pet animals in your community stay safe.

Name _____

> - A **series** is a set of three or more words.
> - Use commas to separate three or more words in a series.
> - The word *and* or *or* comes before the last word in a series.
>   Jill, Kamma, and Lee are coming over.
>   We can play softball, basketball, or soccer.
> - **Direct address** is when the name of the person being spoken to is included in the sentence.
> - Use a comma to separate the name in direct address.
>   Come in, Oscar.   Dad, can you help me?

A. Write the correct sentence on the line.

1. We have played football dodgeball and tennis.

_____

2. Kayla, do you want a red ball a green ball or a yellow ball?

_____

B. Write two sentences that contain a series. Be sure to add the commas in each series.

3. _____

4. _____

Name_____

> • A noun names a person, place, or thing.
>
> • A **series** is a set of three or more words.
>
> • Commas separate the words in a series.
>
> • The word *and* or *or* comes before the last word in a series.

A. Read the passage. Insert commas where they are needed. Write the corrected passage on the lines.

Birds make nests from sticks grass and straw. Some birds also use feathers mud and string. Nests keep birds safe from cold rain or wind.

_____

_____

_____

_____

B. Now find six nouns in the passage. Write them on the lines below.

_____ _____

_____ _____

_____ _____

Name _____

A. Underline the nouns in each sentence.

1. Animals live in many places.

2. The boys like to watch the squirrel.

3. The nuts fell on the ground.

4. The bird flew to a tree.

5. A rabbit lives near my house.

B. Circle the nouns that name a person.

6. The vet petted our rabbit.

7. The artist often paints ducks.

8. His brother is our coach.

Writing/Spelling Connection

Look back through your writer's notebook for nouns you have used. Find some that name people, some that name places, and some that name things.

Name _____

Content words are words that are specific to a field of study. Words like mammal, litter, and omnivore are science content words.

Sometimes you can figure out what a content word means by using context clues.

COLLABORATE **Go on a word hunt with a partner. Find content words related to animals. Write them in the chart.**

Science
_____ _____
_____ _____
_____ _____

CONNECT TO CONTENT

"Eagles and Eaglets" gives facts about how eagles grow. The author uses content words that help you understand the topic.

Circle two words that you were able to figure out the meaning to using context clues. Write the words and what they mean on the lines.

_____

_____

_____

_____

Name _____

Use a word from the box that matches the definition.

secret	spend	customer	choose
tools	fair	rescue	scurries

1. To save from danger or harm _____

2. Treating others in a just and honest way _____

3. Goes or moves in a hurry _____

4. A person who buys something or uses the services of a business

_____

5. To take from what is available _____

6. Known to oneself or a few others _____

7. Things made to help people do work _____

8. To pay money _____

Name _____

Listen to each word your teacher says. Take away the sound. Circle the picture of the new word you made.

1.

2.

3.

4.

5.

Teacher Directions: Explain to children that we can take away a sound from a word to make a new word. Model item 1 by saying *pants. I can take away /p/ from the beginning of* pants *to make a new word: /aaannntsss/,* ants. Guide children to circle the picture of the ants. 2. Say *snail.* Tell children to take away /s/ from the beginning of *snail.* 3. Say *feet.* Tell children to take away /f/ from the beginning of *feet.* 4. Say *clamp.* Tell children to take away /k/ from the beginning of *clamp.* 5. Say *brain.* Tell children to take away /b/ from the beginning of *brain.*

Name _____

Say the picture name. Then say the sounds in the word one at a time. Draw an X in the box for each sound you hear. Write the number of sounds on the line.

1.

2.

3.

4.

5.

Teacher Directions: Model 1. *I can say the sounds in the word* mow *The word* mow *has two sounds: /m/ /ō/. Say the sounds with me.* Guide children to draw 2 X's and write the number of sounds for #1.

Name _____

> The short ***u*** sound you hear in ***cub*** is spelled with ***u***. The long ***u*** sound you hear in ***fuse*** can be spelled with ***u_e***.
>
> **cub**   **fuse**
>
>   

A. Look at each picture. Read the words and circle the one that names the picture. Write the word.

1.
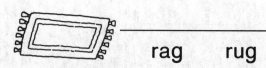
_____

rag   rug

2.

_____

mule   mole

3.
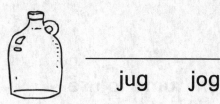
_____

jug   jog

4.
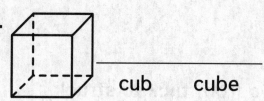
_____

cub   cube

B. Write a word from the box to complete each sentence.

> cute   mug   pumpkin   confuse

5. The _____ is huge.

6. Our new puppy is _____.

7. His _____ is hot.

8. The rules of the game _____ me.

Name _____

> Listen to the sound in the middle of the word *cube*. The **e** at the end of the word gives the letter **u** the long **u** sound.

1. Go from **clump** to **bump**

2. Go from **cute** to **mule**

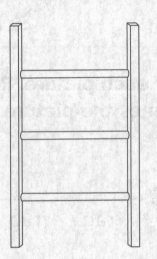

3. Go from **tuck** to **struck**

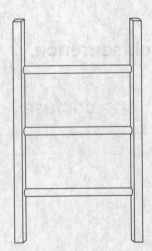

4. Go from **fume** to **use**

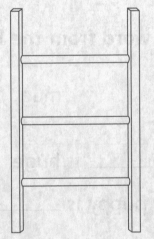

Name _____

Some words can be split into two syllables. Sometimes one syllable has a consonant, a vowel, a consonant and a final *e*. These are called CVCe syllables. Usually these syllables have a long vowel sound and the final *e* is silent.

ni<u>ne</u>ty # 90

A. Write a CVCe word to name each picture. Draw a line between the syllables. Circle the CVCe syllable.

1. _____ 2. _____

3. _____ 4. _____

B. Split these words into two syllables. Circle the CVCe syllable.

5. combine _____

6. impose _____

7. define _____

8. useful _____

9. refuse _____

Name _____

Complete each sentence. Use the words in the box.

fall	look	won	change	should
yes	their	five	open	cheer

1. We went to meet _____ friends.

2. Do not _____ your socks yet.

3. We will _____ when they win the game.

4. They _____ the game.

5. Try not to _____ off the deck.

6. _____, we ate on the deck.

7. My sister is _____ years old.

8. We _____ go get some water.

9. When does the store _____?

10. We will _____ for your glasses.

Name _____

Fold back the paper along the dotted line. Use the blanks to write each word as it is read aloud. When you finish the test, unfold the paper. Use the list at the right to correct any spelling mistakes.

Review Words

High-Frequency Words

1. _____
2. _____
3. _____
4. _____
5. _____
6. _____
7. _____
8. _____
9. _____
10. _____
11. _____
12. _____
13. _____
14. _____
15. _____

1. mule
2. fuse
3. plum
4. use
5. dug
6. cub
7. cute
8. hum
9. must
10. fun
11. rope
12. nose
13. look
14. yes
15. their

Name _____

mule	fuse	plum	use	dug
cub	hum	cute	must	fun

A. Write the spelling words that have the short *u* sound as in *up*.

1. _____   2. _____   3. _____

4. _____   5. _____   6. _____

B. Write the spelling words that have the long *u* sound as in *fume*.

7. _____   8. _____

9. _____   10. _____

C. Read each group of words. Circle the words that have the same vowel sound.

11. cub   plum   use

12. hum   cute   fuse

13. must   use   dug

14. fun   fuse   hum

15. use   cute   cub

Name _____

---

mule   fuse   but   use   bug

cub   hum   cute   mud   fun

A. Write the spelling words that have the short *u* sound as in *up*.

1. _____   4. _____

2. _____   5. _____

3. _____   6. _____

B. Write the spelling words that have the long *u* sound as in *fume*.

7. _____   9. _____

8. _____   10. _____

C. Read each group of words. Circle the words that have the same vowel sound.

11. mule   hum   use   14. fun   bug   cute

12. cub   mud   fuse   15. fuse   hum   mud

13. bug   fuse   mule

Name _____

mules	fuse	plums	cubs	dug
dusted	hummed	cute	trusting	drums

A. Write the spelling words that have the short *u* sound as in *up*.

1. _____   5. _____

2. _____   6. _____

3. _____   7. _____

4. _____

B. Write the spelling words that have the long *u* sound as in *fume*.

8. _____   10. _____

9. _____

C. Read each group of words. Circle the words that have the same vowel sound.

11. trusting dug   fuse   14. mules   hummed cubs

12. mules cute drums   15. fuse   cute   dug

13. cubs   huge plums

Name _____

- A **singular noun** names one person, place, or thing.
- A **plural noun** names more than one person, place, or thing.
- Add **-s** to make the plural of most nouns.

    I see one <u>cat</u>.

    You see two <u>cats</u>.

Make the underlined noun plural. Write it on the line provided.

1. The fox saw the <u>grape</u> in a tree. _____

2. The fox took the <u>step</u> to reach them. _____

3. The rabbit ate the <u>carrot</u>. _____

4. The farmer saw the golden <u>egg</u>. _____

5. The <u>bird</u> flew over the trees. _____

6. The cat liked to chase the <u>dog</u>. _____

 Use the sentences as a model. Write about how different kinds of animals find food.

Name _____

> • Add **-s** to make the plural of most nouns.
> • Add **-es** to form the plural of singular nouns that end in **s**, **ch**, **sh**, or **x**.
>
>   wish → wishes   box → boxes
>
> • To form the plural of nouns ending in a consonant and **y**, change the **y** to **i** and add **-es**.
>
>   story → stories

Complete each sentence with the nouns in ( ). Write the nouns in their plural forms.

1. The shepherd boy made up many _____. (story)

2. He saw _____, dragons, and dogs in the sky. (fox)

3. One of his _____ was to watch the sheep. (duty)

4. One of the sheep had several _____. (baby)

5. A wolf hid in the _____. (bush)

Name _____

- An **abbreviation** is a shortened form of a word. It begins with a capital letter and ends with a period. Street names are often abbreviated.

  Street → St.   Avenue → Ave.   Drive → Dr.   Road → Rd.

- The abbreviation of a **title** before a name begins with a capital letter and ends with a period. First and last names are proper nouns and begin with capital letters.

  Dr. Allen   Mrs. Lucas   Ms. Jennifer Bailey

A. Write each name and abbreviation correctly.

1. mr mark adams

_____

2. dr sally gordon

_____

3. ms amy smith

_____

4. mrs. mary jones

_____

B. Write each address using an abbreviation.

5. 245 Oak Street

_____

6. 563 Hill Avenue

_____

7. 749 Wilson Drive

_____

8. 322 Valley Road

_____

Name _____

- Add *-s* to make the plural of most nouns.
- Add *-es* to form the plural of singular nouns that end in *s*, *ch*, *sh*, or *x*.
- To form the plural of nouns ending in a consonant and *y*, change the *y* to *i* and add *-es*.

Draw a line below each mistake in the paragraph. Then rewrite the paragraph correctly on the lines.

A fox saw some berrys. They were high in a tree. He ran and jumped to try to get them. The branchs were too high. He told the other foxs, "They must taste bad."

_____

_____

_____

What wild animals live in your community? Explain ways that the people in your community can help the wild animals who live nearby.

Name _____

Complete each sentence with the nouns in ( ). Write the nouns in their plural forms.

1. There are many _____ about animals. (fable).

2. One of the _____ is about an ant. (story)

3. The ant gathered _____ of wheat. (grain)

4. He stored the food for his _____. (baby)

5. A grasshopper spent his _____ playing. (day)

6. When winter came, the ant _____ had food. (family)

7. The grasshopper begged for wheat, rice, or _____.

   (berry)

8. He had no food for his _____. (lunch)

| Writing/Spelling Connection | **Look back through your writer's notebook for plural nouns you used. Check that you used them correctly.** |

Name _____

Homographs are words that are spelled the same but have different meanings. They may sound different, or they may sound the same.

Read each sentence. Choose the definition that fits the homograph in bold print. Write it on the line.

1. It **does** look like it's going to rain.

   two female deer   a form of the verb "to do"

   _____

2. Watch how I swing my **bat** at the ball.

   a small animal with wings   a long stick used in baseball

   _____

3. He tied the ribbon into a **bow**.

   two loops tied together   to bend at the waist

   _____

4. She showed me how to **row** the boat.

   a line   to use oars to move

   _____

5. We have no **use** for the extra blanket.

   a purpose   to put into action

   _____

Name _____

One way to learn what a new word means is to look it up in a dictionary. A **dictionary** lists all the words in the English language in alphabetical order.

• The **entry words** show the spelling and syllables of each word.

• The **pronunciation** of each word is shown in parentheses.

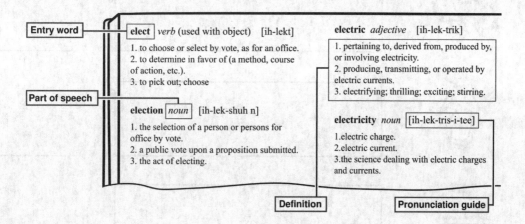

Entry word

elect *verb* (used with object)   [ih-lekt]
1. to choose or select by vote, as for an office.
2. to determine in favor of (a method, course of action, etc.).
3. to pick out; choose

Part of speech

election *noun* [ih-lek-shuh n]
1. the selection of a person or persons for office by vote.
2. a public vote upon a proposition submitted.
3. the act of electing.

electric *adjective*   [ih-lek-trik]
1. pertaining to, derived from, produced by, or involving electricity.
2. producing, transmitting, or operated by electric currents.
3. electrifying; thrilling; exciting; stirring.

electricity *noun*   [ih-lek-tris-i-tee]
1.electric charge.
2.electric current.
3.the science dealing with electric charges and currents.

Definition   **Pronunciation guide**

Use the dictionary entry and context clues to help you figure out the meaning of each word in bold.

1. You can use the **electric** can opener to open the can of beans.

_____

2. The game was **electric**.

_____

Say each word in the dictionary entry out loud with a partner. How many syllables are in each word? How do you know?

Name _____

Say the picture name. Then say the sounds in the word one at a time. Draw an X in the box for each sound you hear. Write the number of sounds on the line.

1.

2.

3.

4.

5.

6.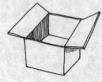

Teacher Directions: 1. Model: *I can say the sounds in the word* pot. *The word* pot *has three sounds:* /p/ /o/ /t/. *Say the sounds with me.* Guide children to draw 3 X's and write the number of sounds for #1.

Name _____

Listen to the word your teacher says. Change the sound. Circle the picture of the new word you made.

1.

2.

3.

4.

5.

Teacher Directions: 1. Model: *This is the picture for the word* phone. *I can change the first sound /f/ to /k/ to make a new word. Listen to the new word:* cone. *I will circle the picture for the word* cone. **2.** Say *mice.* Change /m/ to /d/. **3.** Say *racket.* Change /r/ to /j/. **4.** Say *king.* Change /k/ to /r/. **5.** Say *page.* Change /p/ to /k/.

Name _____

Sometimes the letter _c_ stands for the _s_ sound, as in **fa<u>c</u>e**.

The letter _g_ can stand for the _j_ sound, as in **gel**.

The letters _dge_ can stand for the _j_ sound, as in **fri<u>dge</u>**.

fa<u>c</u>e  **gel**  **fri<u>dge</u>**

A. Fill in the blank with the word that completes each sentence.

1. A penny is worth one _____.
   a. cent   **b.** can

2. Sam likes _____ball.
   a. dog   **b.** dodge

3. Grace has a book of _____tricks.
   a. magic   **b.** mug

4. My mom has a big _____ in her ring.
   a. gum   **b.** gem

5. Madge has a _____ on her leg.
   a. black   **b.** brace

B. Circle the letters that stand for the _s_ and _j_ sounds in each answer above.

Name _____

Sometimes the letter *c* stands for the *s* sound, as in <u>c</u>ent.

The letter *g* can stand for the *j* sound, as in **gem**.

The letters *dge* can stand for the *j* sound, as in **smu<u>dge</u>**.

<u>c</u>ent   **g**em   smu<u>dge</u>

Read the sentences and words. Circle the word that completes the sentence. Write the word on the line.

1. His cab is on the _____.

cage   bridge   game

2. My dad made _____ for lunch.

rice   grace   fence

3. He has five mice in a _____.

cage   rice   ice

4. Pam is _____.

face   rice   nice

5. Do not cut the _____ too short.

binge   hedge   singe

6. We live in the _____.

hinge   pencil   city

7. The polar bear dove into the _____ water.

frigid   giant   singe

Name _____

> A **prefix** is a word part added to the beginning of a word
> to change its meaning.
> The prefix *un-* means "not."
> The prefix *re-* means "again."
> The prefix *dis-* means "opposite of."
>
> <u>un</u>lock   <u>re</u>act   <u>dis</u>place

A. Match each sentence to a word with a prefix. Use the underlined words to help you.

1. I will <u>use</u> the bag <u>again</u>.   **a.** unlocked

2. Ken will <u>fill</u> the fish tank <u>again</u>.   **b.** dislike

3. She left the door <u>not locked</u>.   **c.** reuse

4. He is <u>not wise</u>.   **d.** refill

5. What I feel is the <u>opposite of</u> <u>like</u>.   **e.** unwise

B. Add a prefix to the underlined word to tell the meaning of the two words. Write the new word on the line.

6. <u>play</u> again _____

7. not <u>able</u> _____

8. opposite of <u>trust</u> _____

9. not <u>safe</u> _____

Name _____

Complete each sentence. Use the words in the box.

almost	buy	food	out	pull
saw	sky	straight	under	wash

1. They _____ the new film.

2. I left the key _____ the mat.

3. We will cook the _____ for the party.

4. He walked _____ of the room.

5. We _____ the dishes after dinner.

6. The balloon drifted into the _____.

7. The team _____ won the game.

8. You must _____ the cord to start the motor.

9. That road is _____.

10. Mom will _____ us dinner.

Name _____

Fold back the paper
along the dotted line.
Use the blanks to write
each word as it is read
aloud. When you finish
the test, unfold the
paper. Use the list at
the right to correct any
spelling mistakes.

1. _____
2. _____
3. _____
4. _____
5. _____
6. _____
7. _____
8. _____
9. _____
10. _____

Review Words

11. _____
12. _____

**High-Frequency
Words**

13. _____
14. _____
15. _____

1. trace
2. place
3. badge
4. cage
5. space
6. ice
7. bulge
8. range
9. edge
10. mice
11. mule
12. huge
13. out
14. wash
15. saw

Name _____

trace	place	badge	cage	space
ice	bulge	range	edge	mice

A. Write the spelling words that have the soft *c* sound, as in *spice*.

1. _____ 2. _____ 3. _____

4. _____ 5. _____

B. Write the spelling words that have the soft *g* sound, as in *page*.

6. _____ 7. _____ 8. _____

9. _____ 10. _____

C. Read each group of words. Circle the words that have the same end sound.

11. place   edge   trace

12. ice   badge   bulge

13. mice   space   range

14. cage   bulge   place

15. edge   trace   ice

Name _____

rice	mice	badge	cage	race
ice	bulge	range	edge	space

A. Write the spelling words that have the soft c sound, as in _spice_.

1. _____   4. _____

2. _____   5. _____

3. _____

B. Write the spelling words that have the soft g sound as in _page_.

6. _____   9. _____

7. _____   10. _____

8. _____

C. Read each group of words. Circle the words that have the same end sound.

11. bulge   edge   space   14. range   ice   cage

12. badge   rice   cage   15. bulge   ice   mice

13. cage   race   space

Name _____

| race | placed | badges | cage | space |
| ice | bulge | range | edges | racing |

A. Write the spelling words that have the soft *c* sound, as in *spice*.

1. _____   4. _____

2. _____   5. _____

3. _____

B. Write the spelling words that have the soft *g* sound as in *page*.

6. _____   9. _____

7. _____   10. _____

8. _____

C. Read each group of words. Circle the words that have the same end sound.

11. badges   edges   space   14. range   ice   cage

12. bulge   racing   cage   15. bulge   ice   space

13. placed   bulge   range

Name _____

> - A **common noun** names any person, place, or thing.
> - A **proper noun** names a special person, place, or thing.
> - A proper noun begins with a capital letter.
>
>   Polar bears live near the <u>Arctic Circle</u>.
>
>   Bats sleep in caves all over the <u>United States</u>.

A. Circle the proper nouns.

1. Many frogs live on the banks of the Mississippi River.

2. Ducks can be found in wetlands across North America.

3. Many buffalo live in the grasslands of Montana.

4. Many fish swim in Walden Pond.

5. Some crocodiles live in the Florida Everglades.

B. Underline the common nouns in the sentences above. List them on the lines below.

_____   _____

_____   _____

_____   _____

_____   _____

 Use the sentences as a model. Write about a group of animals you have seen. Use common, proper, and collective nouns.

Name _____

> • A **collective noun** names a group of people, places, or things.
>
> a <u>flock</u> of sheep
>
> a <u>herd</u> of deer
>
> a <u>team</u> of baseball players

Circle the collective nouns.

1. The flock of geese flew over our heads.

2. A herd of cows is grazing in the field.

3. Jack saw a school of fish in the river.

4. Mary fixed a basket for the litter of puppies.

5. A pack of wolves ran through the forest.

6. A swarm of bees buzzed near the flowers.

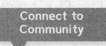 **Connect to Community** Explain some ways to improve your environment to help future generations of animals in your area.

Name _____

> • Some proper nouns name days of the week, months, and holidays.
> • The name of each day, month, or holiday begins with a capital letter.
>   <u>S</u>unday   <u>J</u>une   <u>F</u>ather's <u>D</u>ay
> • Abbreviations for the days of the week or the months of the year begin with a capital letter and end with a period.
>   Monday → Mon.   December → Dec.

A. Choose the proper noun that names a day, month, or holiday. Write it correctly on the line below.

1. september
fall
school

_____

2. vote
flag
veterans' day

_____

3. afternoon
night
thursday

_____

4. summer
labor day
fun

_____

B. Write the correct abbreviation for each proper noun.

5. February _____   **6.** Tuesday _____

7. Saturday _____   **8.** April _____

Name _____

- The names of the days of the week, the months of the year, and holidays are proper nouns and begin with a capital letter.
- Use a **comma** between the day and the year.
  January 24, 2005

Draw a line below each mistake. Then rewrite the letter.

october 1 2006

Dear wendy,

My class read about sea turtles on monday. I would like to see pictures of sea turtles from florida. Please send them to me in idaho.

Your friend,
tony

_____

_____

_____

_____

Name _____

Read the underlined word. Circle the word that shows what kind of noun it is.

1. The penguins came from <u>Antarctica</u>.

   common   proper

2. Some birds were building <u>nests</u>.

   common   proper

3. We saw a <u>herd</u> of elephants.

   proper   collective

4. The <u>pelicans</u> came from Florida.

   common   proper

5. The <u>flock</u> of sheep fed on grass.

   proper   collective

6. Her birthday is in <u>February</u>.

   collective   proper

 Look back through your writer's notebook for common, proper, and collective nouns you have used. Check that you used them correctly.

Name _____

> Expand your vocabulary by adding or removing inflectional endings, prefixes, or suffixes to a base word to create different forms of a word.

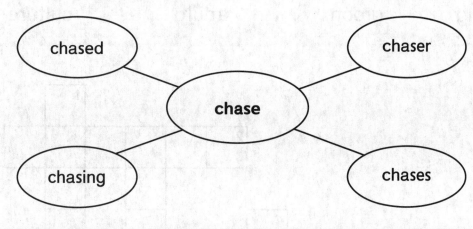

Use your notes from "The Boy Who Cried Wolf." Choose one word and write it in the word web. Add circles to the web to write as many related words as you can. Use a dictionary to help you.

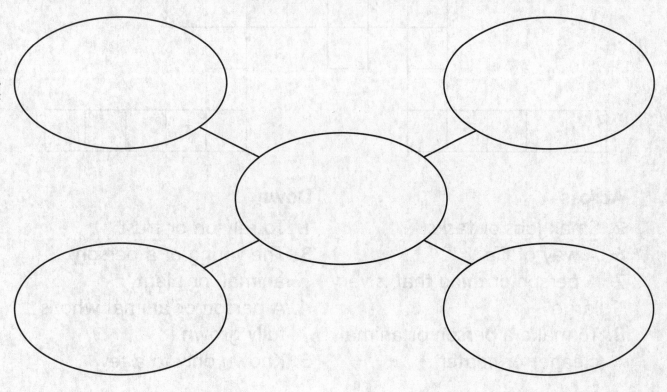

Name _____

Use a word from the box that matches the definition.

depend	chores	giant	secret
offspring	groom	adult	culture

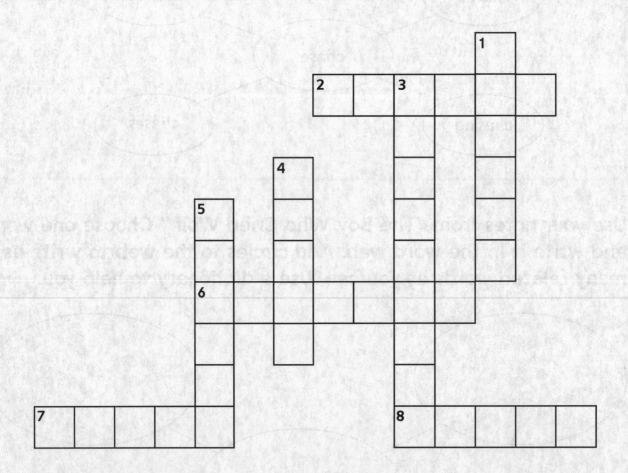

Across

2. Small jobs or tasks
6. A way of life
7. A person or thing that is very large
8. To make a person or animal cleaner or neater

Down

1. To rely on or trust
3. The young of a person, animal, or plant
4. A person or animal who is fully grown
5. Known only to a few

Name_____

Words that rhyme end with the same sounds.

Say the name of each picture. Then draw two pictures of things whose names rhyme with it.

1.

2.

3.

4.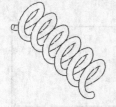

Teacher Directions: Read the box at the top of the page. Point to the pictures as you say *cat, bat,* and *hat.* Emphasize the ending sounds in each word. Point out that all three words rhyme.

Name _____

Say the picture name. Then say the sounds in the word one at a time. Draw an X in the box for each sound you hear. Write the number of sounds on the line.

1.

   _____

2.

   _____

3.

   _____

4.

   _____

5.

   _____

6.

   _____

Teacher Directions: Model 1. *I can say the sounds in the word* slide *The word* slide *has four sounds: /s/ /l/ /ī/ /d/. Say the sounds with me.* Guide children to draw 4 X's and write the number of sounds for #1.

Name _____

Digraphs are groups of letters that stand for a single sound. The letters *sh*, *th*, and *ng* are digraphs.

fi**sh**   **th**ink    ri**ng**

A. Use a word from the box to complete each sentence.

math	shopping	sing	wish	bathtub

1. Chad washes his dog in the _____.

2. This card is a "get well" _____ for Seth.

3. Shane has cash to go _____.

4. That class has a _____ test.

5. Tish likes to _____.

B. Circle the word that names the picture. Underline the digraphs *th*, *sh*, or *-ng*.

6.   wing   wig   7.    ship   sip

8.   path   pat   9.   top   tooth

Name _____

Digraphs and trigraphs are groups of letters that stand for a single sound. The letters *ch*, *-tch*, *wh-*, and *ph* are examples.

chin   crutch   whale phone

A. Circle the word that names each picture. Then write the word on the line.

1. 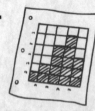 whip while wipe ___	**2.**  shack check chick ___	**3.** which itching chipping ___
4. laugh graph grape ___	**5.**  catches cactus latch ___	**6.**  chap shop chop ___

B. Circle the digraph or trigraph *ch, tch, wh,* or *ph* in each answer above.

Name _____

> A **suffix** is a word part at the end of a word. A suffix changes the meaning of the word.
>
> *-ful* means "full of"   hopeful = full of hope
>
> *-less* means "without"   hopeless = without hope

A. Read each sentence. Underline the word that has the suffix *-ful* or *-less*. Write the word on the line.

1. A rake is a useful thing. _____

2. A little pup is helpless. _____

3. The dishes are spotless. _____

4. We will not be wasteful. _____

B. Read the words. Circle the best meaning for each word.

1. restless   full of rest   without rest

2. skillful   full of skill   without skill

3. trustful   full of trust   without trust

4. useless   full of use   without use

Name _____

Complete each sentence. Use the words in the box.

baby	early	eight	isn't	learn
seven	start	these	try	walk

1. He _____ the best at this game.

2. Please _____ the test now.

3. I will have a _____ sister next year.

4. You should _____ to call later.

5. We will _____ to the park.

6. Mom is _____ years older than Dad.

7. The class can _____ each day.

8. Students wake up _____ each day.

9. Spiders have _____ legs.

10. The family likes _____ apples.

Name _____

Fold back the paper
along the dotted line.
Use the blanks to write
each word as it is read
aloud. When you finish
the test, unfold the
paper. Use the list at
the right to correct any
spelling mistakes.

Review Words

**High-Frequency
Words**

#		#	
1.	_____	1.	chop
2.	_____	2.	catch
3.	_____	3.	shape
4.	_____	4.	trash
5.	_____	5.	phone
6.	_____	6.	that
7.	_____	7.	sting
8.	_____	8.	thin
9.	_____	9.	bring
10.	_____	10.	while
11.	_____	11.	place
12.	_____	12.	badge
13.	_____	13.	seven
14.	_____	14.	isn't
15.	_____	15.	early

Name _____

chop	catch	shape	trash	phone
that	sting	thin	bring	while

A. Write the spelling words that match each consonant digraph.

sh   *ch*   *wh*   *tch*

1. _____   3. _____   4. _____   5. _____

2. _____

th   *ng*   *ph*

6. _____   8. _____   10. _____

7. _____   9. _____

B. Read each group of words. Circle the word that does not fit the pattern.

11. shape, chop, trash   12. phone, thin, that

13. sting, bring, while   14. thin, catch, that

15. trash, shape, sting

Name _____

chop	catch	shape	fish	phone
this	ring	thin	sang	whale

A. Write the spelling words that match each consonant digraph.

sh   **ch**   **wh**   **tch**

1. _____   3. _____   4. _____   5. _____

2. _____

th   **ng**   **ph**

6. _____   8. _____   10. _____

7. _____   9. _____

B. Read **each group of words. Circle the word that does not fit the pattern.**

11. ring   sang   whale

12. shape   catch   fish

13. chop   this   thin

14. shape   whale   fish

15. phone   sang   ring

Name _____

chopped	catches	shapes	trash	phones
that's	sting	thinner	bringing	while

A. Write the spelling words that match each consonant digraph.

sh	*ch*	*wh*	*tch*
1. _____	3. _____	4. _____	5. _____

2. _____

th	*ng*	*ph*
6. _____	8. _____	10. _____

7. _____   9. _____

B. Read each group of words. Circle the word that does not fit the pattern.

11. sting   bringing   while

12. shapes   catches   trash

13. chopped   that's   thinner

14. shapes   while   trash

15. phones   sting   bringing

Name _____

> • A **plural noun** names more than one person, place, or thing.
> • Most nouns add **-s** or **-es** to make their plural form.
> • Some nouns change their spelling to make their plural form.
>
> foot → feet child → children woman → women
>
> tooth → teeth man → men mouse → mice

A. Complete each sentence with the nouns in ( ). Write the nouns in their plural forms.

1. Three _____ took a hike on the path. (child)

2. Two _____ led the hike. (woman)

3. The hike hurt their _____. (foot)

B. Write a sentence using the plural form of the noun in ( ).

4. (mouse)

_____

5. (tooth)

_____

Name _____

> - Some nouns change their spelling from singular to plural.
>
>   mouse → mice   goose → geese
>
> - Some words stay the same.
>
>   deer → deer   fish → fish   sheep → sheep
>
> - The rest of the sentence will show you whether the noun is about one thing or more than one thing.
>
>   Jack caught a fish. (only one fish)
>
>   Two fish are in the bowl. (more than one fish)

Write "one" if the underlined word means one thing. Write "more than one" if it means more than one thing.

1. Max saw a baby <u>sheep</u> under the trees. _____

2. The <u>sheep</u> are in the field. _____

3. The baby <u>deer</u> has little teeth. _____

4. Four <u>deer</u> ran across the path. _____

5. He watched many <u>fish</u> swim. _____

6. I saw him catch a <u>fish</u>. _____

Name _____

> • Use **quotation marks** at the beginning and at the end of the exact words a person says.
>
> • The punctuation at the end of the speaker's words is also included inside the quotation marks.
>
>   "Did you find your game?" Mom asked.
>
>   "Yes," Jen said.

Write each sentence. Add quotation marks where needed.

1. Can Mom and I play your game? Dad asked.

_____

2. Yes, Jen said. But if I win, you have to give me a prize.

_____

3. Dad asked, Do you have to give me a prize if I win?

_____

4. Jen said, If you or Mom win, I will draw a picture for you.

_____

5. Dad said, If you win, we will take you out to dinner.

_____

Name _____

- Some nouns change their spelling from singular to plural.

  foot → feet   person → people

- Some words stay the same.

  fish → fish   sheep → sheep   deer → deer

- The rest of the sentence will show you whether the noun is about one thing or more than one thing.

  A deer stood still in the woods. (only one deer)

  We saw many sheep in the meadow.
  (more than one sheep)

Write "one" if the underlined word means one thing. Write "more than one" if it means more than one thing.

1. Pete saw a <u>sheep</u> by the tree.   _____

2. Five <u>sheep</u> were eating grass.   _____

3. We caught several <u>fish</u> from the river.   _____

4. Sara caught a very large <u>fish</u>.   _____

5. Two <u>deer</u> crossed the road.   _____

 Use the sentences as a model. Write about time you spent in nature with others. Practice using plural nouns.

Name _____

Circle the correct form of the noun to complete each sentence.

1. Several _____ flew over our home.

   geese   gooses   geeses

2. We saw six _____ in the woods.

   deers   deer   deer's

3. Two _____ live in the tree stump.

   mouses   mice   mouse

4. The boys saw an _____ nest in the tree.

   owl   owls   owl's

5. The teacher walked with the _____.

   girls   girl's   girls'

6. The _____ ate dinner under the trees.

   childs   children   child's

7. Only two more _____ plates can fit in the sink.

   person's   people   people's

Connect to Community Write about a park in your community. Include ideas to make the park better.

Writing/Spelling Connection Look back through your writer's notebook for plural nouns you used. Check that you used them correctly.

Name _____

> **Antonyms** are words that have opposite meanings. For example, the words *big* and *small* are antonyms.

A. Read each pair of sentences. Find the two words that are antonyms. Circle the antonyms.

1. Turn the light off when you leave the room.
   I will turn it back on when I get up.

2. The cars on the big road go very fast.
   But on our street, the cars have to go slowly.

3. It gets very cold here in the winter.
   However, in summer the weather becomes quite hot.

4. I like to wear clothes in dark colors.
   My sister likes light colors better.

B. Write an antonym of the word in ( ) to complete each sentence.

5. Those mountains are very _____ . (short)

6. When the light turns red, the cars _____ . (start)

7. Brad asked us to be _____ in here. (loud)

Name _____

> To figure out a new word, separate the **base word** from the ending. When added to verbs, the endings **-s, -es,** and **-ing** mean the action is happening now. The ending **-ed** means the action happened in the past.

Read each sentence. Look at each underlined word. Draw a line between the base word and the ending. Then write the meaning of the word.

1. He <u>lives</u> in the city.

_____

2. Fifty firefighters lived and <u>worked</u> there, too.

_____

3. He <u>helped</u> the dog learn to live in the fire station.

_____

4. Then the firefighter <u>takes</u> the dog home.

_____

5. He also has fun <u>meeting</u> and playing with other dogs.

_____

Name _____

Words that rhyme end with the same sounds.

A. Look at the row of pictures. Circle the two pictures whose names rhyme.

1.

2.

B. Look at each picture. Then draw two more pictures of things whose names rhyme with it.

3.

4.

Name _____

Listen to the sounds your teacher says. Blend the sounds to make a word. Circle the picture that goes with that word.

Teacher Directions: Model item 1 by saying /th/ /r/ /ō/ /n/. *Listen as I blend these four sounds:* /thrrrōōōnnn/, throne. *I blended the word* throne. *Say it with me. I'll circle the picture of the* throne. For items 2-5, have children listen to the sounds, blend them to form a word, and circle the correct picture. 2. /sh/ /r/ /i/ /m/ /p/. 3. /s/ /t/ /r/ /i/ /ng/. 4. /th/ /r/ /ō/ /t/. 5. /s/ /t/ /ā/ /j/.

Name _____

Blends are groups of letters that work together. Some three-letter blends are *str, scr, spr, spl, shr, thr*.

<u>str</u>ing

<u>spl</u>ash

A. Read the words. Circle the one that names each picture.

1. strong **strap** sprig	**2.** stripe **sting** spot	**3.** than **throne** thin
4. splat stretch **split**	**5.** throwing thankful **thrilling**	**6.** sprang **strong** strung
7. scrimp splotch **scratch**	**8.** splatter splendid **splinter**	**9.** **spring** strive scrawl

Name _____

Blends are groups of letters that work together.
Some three-letter blends are *str*, *scr*, *spr*, *spl*, *shr*, *thr*.

st**r**ap   sp**r**ing

Write the missing three-letter blend to finish the picture name.

1. _____ ash

2. _____ etching

3. _____ ubbing

4.  _____ it

5.  _____ ink

6.  _____ ike

Name _____

> A **compound word** is made up of two smaller words.
> Compound words have more than one syllable.
> **sun + shine = sunshine**

Circle the compound word in each row. Draw a line between the two words that make the compound word.

1. handshake   handed   helpful

2. lifted   lifetime   likeness

3. hopeful   remake   homemade

4. camping   cannot   classic

5. brakes   robot   bathrobe

6. landslide   skillful   dislike

7. dismiss   salesman   unplug

8. baseball   thankful   ending

9. rename   sandbag   dismiss

10. backstage   unlatch   wished

Name _____

Complete each sentence. Use the words in the box

bird	far	field	flower	grow
leaves	light	orange	ready	until

1. Can you cut the grass in the _____?

2. I want to wear _____ pants.

3. Ed takes a long time to get _____ for work.

4. The _____ woke me up.

5. This _____ does not like to be in a cage.

6. How _____ can you jump?

7. The stem of the _____ is long.

8. How much longer _____ we go to play?

9. These plants _____ fast!

10. My friends and I like to jump in piles of _____.

Name _____

Fold back the paper along the dotted line. Use the blanks to write each word as it is read aloud. When you finish the test, unfold the paper. Use the list at the right to correct any spelling mistakes.

Review Words

High-Frequency Words

1. _____   **1.** scratch
2. _____   **2.** scrape
3. _____   **3.** spring
4. _____   **4.** throne
5. _____   **5.** stripe
6. _____   **6.** strange
7. _____   **7.** shred
8. _____   **8.** shrub
9. _____   **9.** splash
10. _____   **10.** split
11. _____   **11.** catch
12. _____   **12.** sting
13. _____   **13.** far
14. _____   **14.** flower
15. _____   **15.** until

Name _____

scratch	scrape	spring	throne	stripe
strange	shred	shrub	splash	split

A. Look at the spelling words in the box. Match each spelling word to a word below that begins with the same three-letter blend. Write the words on the lines.

scrap

strap

splint

1. _____

3. _____

5. _____

2. _____

4. _____

6. _____

shrug

sprint

thrill

7. _____

9. _____

10. _____

8. _____

B. A letter is missing from each spelling word below. Write the missing letter in the box. Then write the spelling word correctly on the line.

11. sp⬜ash _____

14. t⬜rone _____

12. sh⬜ub _____

15. sc⬜atch _____

13. s⬜red _____

Name _____

scrap	scrape	spring	throne	strip
strike	shred	shrug	splash	split

A. Look at the spelling words in the box. Match each spelling word to a word below that begins with the same three-letter blend. Write the words on the lines.

scrap   strap   splint

1. _____   3. _____   5. _____

2. _____   4. _____   6. _____

shrink   sprint   thrill

7. _____   9. _____   10. _____

8. _____

B. A letter is missing from each spelling word below. Write the missing letter in the box. Then write the spelling word correctly on the line.

11. sp ☐ ash _____   14. sc ☐ ape _____

12. t ☐ rone _____   15. sh ☐ ed _____

13. sh ☐ ug _____

Name _____

| scratch | scraping | spring | throne | striped |
| strange | shreds | shrub | splashes | split |

A. Look at the spelling words in the box. Match each spelling word to a word below that begins with the same three-letter blend. Write the words on the lines.

scrap	strap	splint
1. _____	3. _____	5. _____
2. _____	4. _____	6. _____

shrug	sprint	thrill
7. _____	9. _____	10. _____

8. _____

B. A letter is missing from each spelling word below. Write the missing letter in the box. Then write the spelling word correctly on the line.

11. sp ☐ ashes _____   14. sc ☐ aping _____

12. t ☐ rone _____   15. sh ☐ eds _____

13. sh ☐ ub _____

Name _____

> • A **possessive noun** shows who or what owns something.
> • Add an **apostrophe** (') and **-s** to a singular noun to make it possessive.
>
>   I walk <u>the dog of my friend</u>.   I walk <u>my friend's dog</u>.
>
>   The <u>bowl of the fish</u> is round.   The <u>fish's bowl</u> is round.

Rewrite the underlined parts with a possessive noun. Write it on the line.

1. The <u>dish of the cat</u> is empty. _____

2. The <u>hump of the camel</u> is big. _____

3. <u>The dog of Mia</u> likes to run. _____

4. That cave could be a <u>home of a bat</u>. _____

5. The <u>skin of the snake</u> is very scaly. _____

6. The <u>fur of the cat</u> is very soft. _____

7. <u>The goldfish of Alice</u> is a very quiet pet. _____

 Use the sentences as a model. Write about something that belongs to someone else. Practice using possessive nouns as you write.

Name _____

> • Add just an apostrophe to most **plural nouns** to make them **possessive**.
>
>   We could see the <u>turtles' shells</u>.
>
> • Add an apostrophe and an -*s* to form the possessive of plural nouns that do not end in -*s*.
>
>   The <u>mice's home</u> is in the barn.

Underline the correct plural possessive noun in ( ). Rewrite the sentence on the line below.

1. The (bird's/birds') beaks are full of straw.

_____

2. The (childrens'/children's) favorite animal was the fox.

_____

3. The (duck's/ducks') nests were by the water.

_____

4. The (squirrels'/squirrel's) tails helped them keep warm.

_____

5. The (dog's/dogs') tails are wagging.

_____

Name _____

> • Always use an apostrophe to form a possessive.
> • Add an **apostrophe** and an *s* to make a singular noun possessive.
> • Add an **apostrophe** after the final *s* to make most plural nouns possessive.

Circle the correct form of the possessive nouns in parentheses.

1. The (turtle's/turtles') shells protect them from enemies.

2. A (pig's/pigs') nose is flat.

3. The (cat's/cats') bells are on their collars.

4. A (puppy's/puppies') fur is long and soft.

5. The (dog's/dogs) food is near its bowl.

6. The (cub's/cubs') mother pushed them to the water.

Connect to Community Write about the animals that are in your community.

Name _____

- Add an apostrophe and -*s* to make a singular noun possessive.
- Add an apostrophe to make plural nouns that end in *s* possessive.
- Add an apostrophe and -*s* to plural nouns that do not end in *s*.

Circle the mistakes in the paragraph. Rewrite the paragraph correctly on the lines.

A bats wings are not covered with feathers. Bats wings are made of layers of skin. Their bodies have fur, like mices bodies. A bat that is looking for food sends out little noises. The noises bounce off of an insects body. The bouncing noises help the bat find and eat the bug. Bats fly at night because the suns light would dry out their wings.

_____

_____

_____

_____

_____

Writing/Spelling Connection

Look back through your writer's notebook for possessive nouns you used. Check that you used them correctly.

Name _____

Mark the sentence that is rewritten correctly. Underline the possessive noun in the correct sentence.

1. The wings of the duck are brown and white.
   ○ The ducks wings are brown and white.
   ○ The duck's wings are brown and white.
   ○ The ducks' wings are brown and white.

2. The humps of the camels make them look tall.
   ○ The camels' humps make them look tall.
   ○ The camel's humps make them look tall.
   ○ The camels humps make them look tall.

3. A nest of a bird holds its eggs.
   ○ A birds nest holds its eggs.
   ○ A birds' nest holds its eggs.
   ○ A bird's nest holds its eggs.

4. The food of these geese lives in the river.
   ○ These geeses food lives in the river.
   ○ These geeses' food lives in the river.
   ○ These geese's food lives in the river.

5. Many poems for children are about animals.
   ○ Many childrens poems are about animals.
   ○ Many children's poems are about animals.
   ○ Many childrens' poems are about animals.

Name _____

> To figure out a new word, look for a **suffix**, or word part added to the end of the word.
>
> The suffix **-ly** means "in a way that is."
>
> The suffix **-y** means "full of."

A. Read each sentence. Underline the word that has a suffix. Then write the word and its meaning.

1. "Those will make a healthy snack," Fox thought.

   _____

2. He should be able to reach the grapes easily.

   _____

3. When Fox was safely back on the ground, he shared the grapes with Turtle.

   _____

4. Those grapes were very tasty!

   _____

B. Write a sentence using each word.

5. sleepy _____

6. sleepily _____

Name _____

Draw lines to match the words with their meanings.

1. covered

2. feast

3. check

4. alive

5. snatch

6. cost

7. mammal

8. jobs

a. Having life; living

b. A kind of animal that is warm-blooded and has a backbone

c. Positions of work

d. With a lid on

e. Test to find out if something is correct

f. The amount of money paid or charged for something

g. A large meal for a special day

h. To grab suddenly or quickly

Name _____

> Words rhyme when they have the same ending sounds.

Say the name of each picture. Then draw two pictures of things whose names rhyme with it.

1.	
2.	
3.	
4.	

Teacher Directions: Read the box at the top of the page. Point to the pictures as you name each one: *cat, hat, acrobat.* Explain that these words rhyme. Read the directions with children.

Name _____

Listen to the sounds your teacher says. Blend the sounds to make a word. Circle the picture that goes with that word.

1.

2.

3.

4.

5.

Teacher Directions: Model item 1 by saying: */hw/ /ā/ /l/. Listen as I blend these sounds: /hwāāāāālllll/, whale. I see a picture that shows a whale so I will circle it.* Guide children to blend the sounds and circle the picture. For items 2-5, have children listen to the sounds, blend them to form a word, and circle the correct picture. 2. /s/ /t/ /r/ /ē/ /m/; 3. /k/ /a/ /t/; 4. /n/ /ō/ /z/; 5. /sh/ /r/ /i/ /m/ /p/.

Name _____

> The letters **ai** and **ay** can stand for the long **a** sound.
> The letters **a, ea,** and **ei** can also stand for the long **a** sound.
>
> b**a**by   st**ea**k    r**ei**ndeer

A. Use a word from the box to complete each sentence.
   Then circle the letters that stand for the long a sound.

| train | daytime | table | break | reins |

1. The _____ runs on the track.

2. Put the food on the _____.

3. If you drop that toy, it will _____.

4. Pull the _____ of the horse to tell it to stop.

5. Bats sleep in the _____ and come out at night.

B. Write the word with the long a sound on the line.

6. cat   hay

7. snail   road   _____

Name _____

> The letters *eigh* and *ey* can also stand for the long *a* sound.
>
> <u>eigh</u>t **8** they

A. Use a word from the box to complete each sentence. Then circle the letters that stand for the long a sound.

pay	mail	weigh	obey	vein

1. We had to _____ for the snack.

2. A scale tells how much you _____.

3. She had to _____ a letter to her dad.

4. You should _____ your mom and dad.

5. I can see a _____ through the skin of your hand.

B. Write the word with the long a sound on the line.

6. baby   apple   _____

7. hat   break   _____

Name _____

A **contraction** is a word that is made from two words. An apostrophe (') replaces the letter or letters that are taken out.

he is = he's   you are = you're

she will = she'll   we have = we've

A. Read the words. Draw a line to match each word pair to its contraction.

1. it is   a. you'll

2. we are   b. we're

3. you will   c. it's

4. they have   d. they've

B. Read each contraction. Circle the correct word pair for each contraction.

5. we'll   we will   we are

6. I've   I will   I have

7. she's   she will   she is

8. they're   they are   they have

Name _____

Complete each sentence. Use the words in the box.

about	around	good	great	idea
often	part	second	two	world

1. I will take _____ of the sandwich.

2. Your sister would like to say _____ night.

3. We will take a trip _____ the world.

4. He finished _____ in the race.

5. The show is _____ to end.

6. Our family goes to the park _____.

7. His good _____ made him smile.

8. We will go on a trip for _____ weeks.

9. Some say she is the best player in the _____.

10. Today is a _____ day.

Name _____

Fold back the paper along the dotted line. Use the blanks to write each word as it is read aloud. When you finish the test, unfold the paper. Use the list at the right to correct any spelling mistakes.

1. _____   1. nail

2. _____   2. train

3. _____   3. main

4. _____   4. hay

5. _____   5. stay

6. _____   6. break

7. _____   7. steak

8. _____   8. weigh

9. _____   9. sleigh

10. _____   10. prey

Review Words   11. _____   11. scrape

12. _____   12. strange

High-Frequency Words   13. _____   13. good

14. _____   14. often

15. _____   15. two

Name _____

nail	train	main	hay	stay
break	steak	weigh	sleigh	prey

A. Look at the spelling words in the box. Fill in the blanks with spelling words that match each vowel digraph.

Write the words with the long a sound spelled *ai*.

1. _____ 2. _____ 3. _____

Write the words with the long a sound spelled *ay*.

4. _____ 5. _____

Write the words with the long a sound spelled *ea*.

6. _____ 7. _____

Write the words with the long a sound spelled *eigh*.

8. _____ 9. _____

Write the word with the long a sound spelled *ey*.

10. _____

B. Write the missing letter in the box. Then write the spelling word correctly on the line.

11. ma☐n _____ 12. ha☐ _____

13. pre☐ _____ 14. st☐ak _____

15. we☐gh _____

Name _____

sleigh	nail	break	weigh	rain
they	main	day	steak	ray

A. Look at the spelling words in the box. Fill in the blanks with spelling words that match each vowel digraph.

Write the words with the long a sound spelled _ai_.

1. _____ 2. _____ 3. _____

Write the words with the long a sound spelled _ay_.

4. _____ 5. _____

Write the words with the long a sound spelled _ea_.

6. _____ 7. _____

Write the words with the long a sound spelled _eigh_.

8. _____ 9. _____

Write the words with the long a sound spelled _ey_.

10. _____

B. Write the missing letter in the box. Then write the spelling word correctly on the line.

11. ma [ ] n _____ 12. ra [ ] _____

13. the [ ] _____ 14. st [ ] ak _____

15. we [ ] gh _____

Name _____

| staying | weighed | preying | nails | haystack |
| mainland | sleighs | breaking | steaks | train |

A. Look at the spelling words in the box. Fill in the blanks with spelling words that match each vowel digraph.

Write the words with the long a sound spelled *ai*.

1. _____ 2. _____ 3. _____

Write the words with the long a sound spelled *ay*.

4. _____ 5. _____

Write the words with the long a sound spelled *ea*.

6. _____ 7. _____

Write the words with the long a sound spelled *eigh*.

8. _____ 9. _____

Write the words with the long a sound spelled *ey*.

10. _____

B. Write the missing letter in the box. Then write the spelling word correctly on the line.

11. ma ☐ nland _____ 12. sta ☐ ing _____

13. pre ☐ ing _____ 14. st ☐ aks _____

15. we ☐ ghed _____

Name _____

- An **action verb** is a word that shows action.
- An action verb tells what someone or something is doing.
- To find an action verb, ask *What is the person or thing in this sentence doing?*

    Rain <u>falls</u> from the sky.

    Sara <u>watches</u> the clouds.

Circle the action verb in each sentence. Write it on the line.

1. I toss a ball in the air. _____

2. Gravity pulls the ball down. _____

3. Jessica spills pins on the floor. _____

4. A magnet lifts up the pins. _____

5. Chad steps onto a scale. _____

6. The dial points to his weight. _____

 Use the sentences as a model. Write about time you have spent at a park or playground. Use action verbs to explain what you did at the park or on the playground.

Name _____

> • An **action verb** tells about the action in the sentence.
> • Some action verbs tell about actions that are hard to see.
>   Jim <u>enjoys</u> that book about the weather.

Circle the action verb. Then write another sentence using that same verb.

1. Amy thinks about magnets.

_____

2. Tom loves books about space.

_____

3. Bill listens to a talk about motion.

_____

4. Cara enjoys experiments with gravity.

_____

5. Rita dreams about science.

_____

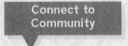 Write about an invention that will help your community. Use action verbs to tell how it will help.

Name _____

> • The first word and each important word in a book title begins with a capital letter.
> • The title of a book is underlined.
>   <u>The Weather Today</u>
>   <u>Let's Watch the Weather!</u>

Write the underlined book title correctly on the lines provided.

1. <u>Blizzards and hurricanes</u> is a book about the weather.

_____

2. I just finished reading a book called <u>the weather and you</u>.

_____

3. <u>See the storm</u> is a picture book.

_____

4. Maria has a book titled <u>predicting the weather</u>.

_____

5. We read <u>weather science</u> in class today.

_____

6. Jake is reading the book, <u>hurricane hints</u>.

_____

Name _____

An action verb tells us what the subject is doing.

A. Circle the action verb in each sentence. Write it on the line.

1. Martin drops the ball. _____

2. The ball rolls down the hill. _____

3. David pushes the swing. _____

4. The swing moves back and forth. _____

5. Jane thinks about trains. _____

6. She learns about them in school. _____

7. Paul enjoys soccer. _____

8. He kicks the ball across the field. _____

B. Write a new sentence using each action verb.

9. brings _____

10. takes _____

11. goes _____

Name _____

Circle the action verb in each sentence. Then write the word on the line.

1. My sister goes to school now. _____

2. I gave her a pen. _____

3. My brother grows flowers. _____

4. He also mows the lawn. _____

5. Ken opens the door. _____

6. My friends play at the table. _____

7. I ate an apple. _____

8. My dad went to the store. _____

9. The cats scratch at the door. _____

10. My brother splashes in the pool. _____

Writing/Spelling Connection

Look back through your writer's notebook for action verbs you have used. Check that you used them correctly. Fix any mistakes you find.

Name _____

Expand your vocabulary by adding or removing inflectional endings, prefixes, or suffixes to a base word to create different forms of a word.

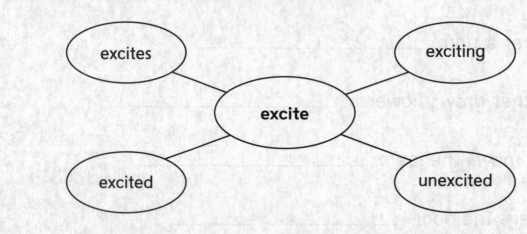

Use your notes from "Lighting Lives." Choose one word and write it in the word web. Add circles to the web to write as many related words as you can. Use a dictionary to help you.

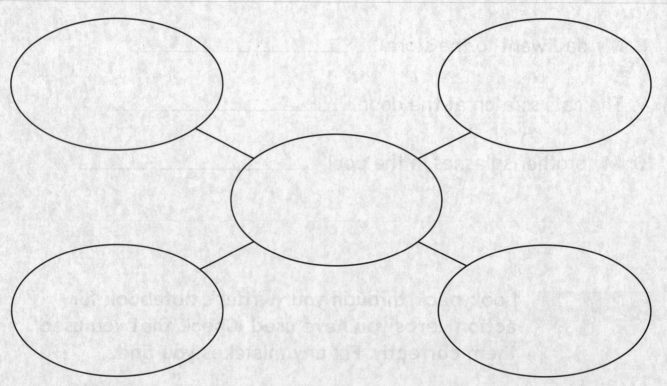

Name _____

Use a word from the box that matches the definition.

believe	remarkable	feathers	stories
choose	lessons	afraid	adult

1. Light, soft body parts that cover a bird's skin _____

2. To decide to take from what is available _____

3. To feel that something is true or real _____

4. A person or animal who is fully grown _____

5. Accounts of things that happened _____

6. Worth talking about _____

7. Feeling fear; frightened _____

8. Things to be learned or taught _____

Name _____

Say each picture name in the row. Say the ending sound. Circle the picture with the same ending sound as the first picture in the row.

Teacher Directions: Model item 1 by saying *This is pan,* /p/ /a/ /n/. Emphasize the ending sound. Then say *bus, mop,* and *sun* and explicitly compare ending sounds. Say: *The words* pan *and* sun *have the same ending sound: /n/.* Bus *and* mop *have different ending sound: /s/ and /p/.* Guide children to circle the picture of the sun.

Name _____

Listen to the word your teacher says. Change the sound in the middle to the new sound your teacher says. Circle the picture of the new word.

1.

2.

3.

4.

5.

Teacher Directions: 1. Model Point to the picture and say: *This is a* mop. *I can change the /o/ in* mop *to /a/. The new word is* map. Guide children to circle the picture. Have them do the following. 2. *pen;* change /e/ to /a/ 3. *gate;* change /ā/ to /ō/ 4. *stamp;* change /a/ to /u/ 5. *cat;* change /a/ to / ī/.

Name _____

Some words have a long *i* sound. Listen to the vowel sound in the words *pie* and *night*. The letters *i, igh, ie,* or *y* can stand for this sound.

pie   night

A. Circle the picture that matches the word. Underline the letters that stand for the long *i* sound.

 1.

sky

2.

flight

 3.

tie

4.

child

B. Read each word below. Find a word from the box that rhymes. Write the word.

| skies | might | wild | pried | remind | reply |

5. July _____

6. tries _____

7. light _____

8. mild _____

9. cried _____

10. behind _____

Name _____

Sights at Night

Dwight takes photos of the night sky. It is his job to spy in the sky. At night, Dwight can find the best sights. When it is nighttime, Dwight tries to spy high in the sky. Dwight might get a fine shot this night! The sky is just right!

Dwight unties his tripod and places it upright. He looks up. The moon and stars shine bright and high. Dwight snaps five shots. The camera flash is bright. The light from the flash makes the foxes hide in fright. Why, it is quite a sight! He snaps ten shots.

It is time for Dwight to drive home. The photos are just right!

1. Circle all the words with long _i_.

2. Complete the sentences.

Dwight takes photos of _____.

At night, Dwight can find the best _____.

Name _____

When a syllable ends in a vowel, the vowel sound is usually long. This type of syllable is called an **open syllable**. The first syllable in *robot* is *ro.* This is an open syllable with a long *o* sound.

A. Read each word. Then draw a line between the syllables. Write each syllable on the line.

1. cozy _____ _____

2. secret _____ _____

3. silent _____ _____

4. donut _____ _____

5. human _____ _____

B. Use the correct word from above to answer each riddle.

6. I am a treat with a hole. I am a _____.

7. I make no sound. I am _____.

8. I am a person. I am a _____.

9. Do not tell. I am a _____.

10. I am soft and warm. I am _____.

Name _____

Complete each sentence. Use the words in the box.

also	apart	begin	either	hundred
over	places	those	which	without

1. Can you see _____ the wall?

2. I ate a plum and _____ a banana.

3. My grandma is almost a _____ years old.

4. He likes _____ pictures better than these.

5. I like to go on trips to _____ far from home.

6. How far _____ do your two friends live?

7. We will _____ when all of us are ready.

8. The ball is in _____ that box or this one.

9. You can pick _____ pen you want.

10. I go _____ a jacket when it is hot.

Name _____

Fold back the paper along the dotted line. Use the blanks to write each word as it is read aloud. When you finish the test, unfold the paper. Use the list at the right to correct any spelling mistakes.

1. _____   **1.** light

2. _____   **2.** sight

3. _____   **3.** mind

4. _____   **4.** cry

5. _____   **5.** tie

6. _____   **6.** high

7. _____   **7.** wild

8. _____   **8.** dry

9. _____   **9.** try

10. _____   **10.** lie

Review Words

11. _____   **11.** hay

12. _____   **12.** steak

High-Frequency Words

13. _____   **13.** begin

14. _____   **14.** those

15. _____   **15.** apart

Name _____

light	sight	mind	cry	tie
high	wild	dry	try	lie

A. Follow the directions to sort the spelling words.

Write the spelling words that have the long *i* sound spelled *i*.

1. _____   2. _____

Write the spelling words that have the long *i* sound spelled *y*.

3. _____   4. _____   5. _____

Write the spelling words that have the long *i* sound spelled *igh*.

6. _____   7. _____   8. _____

Write the spelling words that have the long *i* sound spelled *ie*.

9. _____   10. _____

B. In each spelling word, draw a line through the letter that does not belong. Write the correct spelling word on the line.

11. highe _____   12. miend _____

13. crye _____   14. tyie _____

15. sieght _____

Name _____

pie	right	mind	cry	tie
high	wild	dry	my	find

A. Follow the directions to sort the spelling words.

Write the spelling words that have the long *i* sound spelled *i*.

1. _____   2. _____   3. _____

Write the spelling words that have the long *i* sound spelled *y*.

4. _____   5. _____   6. _____

Write the spelling words that have the long *i* sound spelled *igh*.

7. _____   8. _____

Write the spelling words that have the long *i* sound spelled *ie*.

9. _____   10. _____

B. In each spelling word, draw a line through the letter that does not belong. Write the correct spelling word on the line.

11. highe _____   12. crye _____

13. rieght _____   14. miend _____

15. tyie _____

Name _____

---

lightning	sight	minds	kindness	child
highway	skies	drying	trying	lie

A. Follow the directions to sort the spelling words.

Write the spelling words that have the long *i* sound spelled *i*.

1. _____ 2. _____ 3. _____

Write the spelling words that have the long *i* sound spelled *y*.

4. _____ 5. _____

Write the spelling words that have the long *i* sound spelled *igh*.

6. _____ 7. _____ 8. _____

Write the spelling words that have the long *i* sound spelled *ie*.

9. _____ 10. _____

B. In each spelling word, draw a line through the letter that does not belong. Write the correct spelling word on the line.

11. higheway _____ 12. dryeing _____

13. sieght _____ 14. miends _____

15. lyie _____

Name _____

> • The **tense** of a verb tells when the action takes place.
> • **Present-tense verbs** tell about actions that happen now.
> • The verb form changes to agree with a singular subject. Add **-s** to most verbs if the subject is singular, except when the subject is *I* or *you*.
>
>   Kelly <u>jumps</u> in a puddle.   We <u>jump</u> in a puddle.

A. Circle each present-tense verb. Write the verb on the line.

1. The boys look at the nighttime sky. _____

2. Phil sees a shooting star. _____

3. The moonlight shines in the sky. _____

4. The stars sparkle at night. _____

B. Write two sentences about the daytime sky. Use present tense-verbs.

5. _____

_____

6. _____

_____

 Use the sentences as a model. Write about what you usually do during lunchtime at school. Use present-tense verbs to explain where you go and what you do.

Name _____

> • A **present-tense verb** must agree with the subject of the sentence. The verb form changes to agree with the subject.
> • Add **-s** to most verbs if the subject is singular, except when the subject is *I* or *you*. Add **-es** to verbs that end with **s, ch, sh,** or **x**.
>   The pinwheel <u>spins</u> in the wind. The boy <u>watches</u>.
> • Do not add **-s** or **-es** if the subject is plural.
>   The boys <u>chase</u> the kite.

Underline the verb that agrees with the subject. Write another sentence using the same verb.

1. Mr. Wilson (teach, teaches) about the sky.

_____

2. The Moon (turn, turns) around the Earth.

_____

3. The light of the sun (shine, shines) on the Moon.

_____

4. Stars (help, helps) me see the path.

_____

 Explain how some people in your community help each other. Use present-tense verbs in your answer.

Name _____

> • Use commas to separate three or more words in a series.
> • Use **and** or **or** before the last word in a series.
>   We studied <u>magnets, gravity, and the wind</u> today.

Rewrite each sentence, inserting commas where they are needed.

1. The girls looked at the Moon the stars and the planets.

   _____

2. A telescope helps you see things on land in the sky, or on the sea.

   _____

   _____

3. Books DVDs and the Internet have information about the sky.

   _____

4. We watch the sky in the spring summer, fall and winter.

   _____

5. Jim Sara and Katie are in the Star Gazers Club.

   _____

Name _____

> • **Present-tense verbs** tell about actions that happen now.
>
> • A present-tense verb must agree with the subject of the sentence.
>
> • Add *-s* to most verbs if the subject is singular, except when the subject is *I* or *you*. Add *-es* to verbs that end with *s, ch, sh,* or *x*. Do not add *-s* or *-es* if the subject is plural.

Draw a line below each mistake in the paragraph. Then rewrite the paragraph correctly on the lines.

I likes to look at the night sky. I goes out with my dad, my sister, and my friend to see the stars. We brings a star book, some chairs, and a flashlight. The Moon, stars, and sky changes during the night. We watches until we are tired.

_____

_____

_____

_____

Writing/Spelling Connection

Look back through your writer's notebook for present-tense verbs you used. Check that they agree with their subjects and follow the spelling rules above. Fix any mistakes you find.

Name _____

Write the correct form of the present-tense verb so that it agrees with the subject.

1. Rose and Jill _____ the night sky. (watch)

2. They _____ for shooting stars. (hunt)

3. Rose's mother _____ a telescope. (bring)

4. A telescope _____ them look at the stars. (help)

5. The girls _____ the Moon. (see)

6. It _____ big and white. (look)

7. A star _____ across the sky. (shoot)

8. It _____ in the darkness. (flash)

Name _____

> **Synonyms** are words that have almost the same meaning.

A. Read each pair of sentences. Find the two words that are synonyms. Circle the synonyms and then write them on the lines.

1. She was very happy to be home.

She was so glad to see her family again.

_____ _____

2. When he was 16, he took a long bike trip.

It was quite a journey for a young man!

_____ _____

3. Now when Doug rides, it may be with a group of children.

The group sets up bike rides for the kids.

_____ _____

B. Read the sentences. Write a word to answer each question.

They weren't sure if it was safe to touch the cat.
Once they were certain it was harmless, they all took turns holding it.

4. Which word in the second sentence is a synonym for *sure*?

_____

5. Which word in the second sentence is a synonym for *safe*?

_____

Name _____

> **Homophones** are words that sound the same but have different spellings and meanings.

Read each sentence. Choose the definition that fits the homophone in bold print. Write it on the line.

1. Each day, she saw that students **threw** away sheets and sheets of paper.

   from one side to another   tossed

   _____

2. The students cheered and went back **to** their rooms.

   in the direction of   the number after one

   _____

3. The class that recycles the most paper in one **week** will win a prize.

   seven days   not strong

   _____

4. She **made** a big wall chart.

   helper with housework   created

   _____

Name _____

Say the picture name. Take away the first sound and say the new word. Circle the picture that shows it.

1.

2.

3.

4.

5.

Teacher Directions: Explain to children that we can take away a sound from a word to make a new word. **Model:** *This is* tie. *I can take away /t/ from the beginning of* tie *to make a new word:* eye. Guide children to circle the picture of the eye. Tell children to complete the other items, taking away the first sound of the word, saying the new word, then circling the picture that shows it.

Name _____

Listen to the word your teacher says. Change the sound at the beginning to the new sound your teacher says. Circle the picture of the new word.

Teacher Directions: 1. Model Point to the picture and say: *This is a* hog. *I can change the /h/ in* hog *to /l/. The new word is* log. Guide children to circle the picture. Have them do the following. 2. *can* change /k/ to /v/ 3. *kitten* change /k/ to /m/ 4. *rocket* change /r/ to /l/ 5. *park* change /p/ to /sh/.

Name _____

> Some words have a long *o* sound. Listen to the vowel sound in the words *cold, snow, goat,* and *toe*. The letters *o, ow, oa,* or *oe* can stand for this sound.
>
> **cold**　　　　**snow**　　　　**goat**　　　　**toe**
>
> 　　　

Choose a word to complete each sentence. Write the word on the line.

1. I have five _____.

　　　　　toes　　toast　　top

2. Our class is _____ pumpkin plants.

　　　　going　　growing　　glowing

3. I don't know if this boat will _____.

　　　　　　　　fat　　float　　foam

4. I need a coat on cold _____days.

　　　　　　snowy　　shadow　　solo

5. My pet is big and _____.

　　　　so　　slow　　doe

Name _____

Let It Snow!

Joan throws on a coat. The coat will protect her,
so Joan will not get cold. Joan goes up the road.
What is this? It's not rain. It is snowing!

"Whoa! Snow in May? No way!"

Joan's classmate, Moe, loans her a hat and mittens.
Joan picks up some snow. She makes a snowball and
throws it. Moe shakes off the snow. He chases Joan. Moe
throws snow. Joan laughs. Joan's face is glowing!

Joan and Moe go up the road. Joan stops to take a break.

"Moe, I like to play in the snow!"

Joan and Moe sing "Let it snow, let it snow!"

1. **Circle the words that have long *o*.**
2. **Complete the sentences.**

Joan throws on a _____.

Moe and Joan like to throw _____.

Name _____

Form a **contraction** with _**not**_ by joining the two words together. Then use an **apostrophe (')** to take the place of _o_ in _**not**_.

has not   hasn_t + (') = hasn't

A. Read the sentences. Write a contraction for the underlined pair of words.

1. We <u>were not</u> awake.   _____

2. Mom <u>is not</u> going to the shop.   _____

3. We <u>have not</u> had rain for days.   _____

4. Gran and Gramps <u>are not</u> home.   _____

B. Fill in the blanks to make each contraction.

5. _____ + _____ = wasn't

6. _____ + _____ = doesn't

7. _____ + _____ = hasn't

8. _____ + _____ = didn't

Name _____

Complete each sentence. Use the words in the box.

better	group	long	more	only
our	started	three	who	won't

1. I ate _____ half of my apple.

2. We _____ go until you are ready.

3. A hundred years is a _____ time.

4. The game _____ a little while ago.

5. My sister and I took _____ dog for a walk.

6. This doll is even _____ than the other one.

7. How many _____ minutes can we stay here?

8. I know _____ we should ask about dinner.

9. When two friends and I went to the park, all _____ of us had fun.

10. All my friends were there with me, so we were a pretty big _____.

Name _____

Fold back the paper along the dotted line. Use the blanks to write each word as it is read aloud. When you finish the test, unfold the paper. Use the list at the right to correct any spelling mistakes.

1. _____   **1.** told

2. _____   **2.** most

3. _____   **3.** float

4. _____   **4.** coat

5. _____   **5.** toast

6. _____   **6.** grow

7. _____   **7.** mow

8. _____   **8.** show

9. _____   **9.** Joe

10. _____   **10.** toe

Review Words   11. _____   **11.** light

12. _____   **12.** mind

High-Frequency Words   13. _____   **13.** only

14. _____   **14.** our

15. _____   **15.** who

Name _____

told	most	float	coat	toast
grow	mow	show	Joe	toe

A. Follow the directions to sort the spelling words.

Write the spelling words that have the long *o* sound spelled *o*.

1. _____   2. _____

Write the spelling words that have the long *o* sound spelled *oa*.

3. _____   4. _____   5. _____

Write the spelling words that have the long *o* sound spelled *ow*.

6. _____   7. _____   8. _____

Write the spelling words that have the long *o* sound spelled *oe*.

9. _____   10. _____

B. A letter is missing from each spelling word below. Write the missing letter in the box. Then write the spelling word correctly on the line.

11. fl ☐ at _____   12. gr ☐ w _____

13. to ☐ _____   14. co ☐ t _____

15. t ☐ ld _____

Name _____

| told | most | road | coat | toast |
| grow | crow | show | Joe | toe |

A. Follow the directions to sort the spelling words.

Write the spelling words that have the long _o_ sound spelled _o_.

1. _____ 2. _____

Write the spelling words that have the long _o_ sound spelled _oa_.

3. _____ 4. _____ 5. _____

Write the spelling words that have the long _o_ sound spelled _ow_.

6. _____ 7. _____ 8. _____

Write the spelling words that have the long _o_ sound spelled _oe_.

9. _____ 10. _____

B. A letter is missing from each spelling word below. Write the missing letter in the box. Then write the spelling word correctly on the line.

11. r☐ad _____ 12. gr☐w _____

13. to☐ _____ 14. co☐t _____

15. m☐st _____

Name _____

know	mostly	floating	cloak	toast
woe	bowl	showed	Joe	stows

A. Follow the directions to sort the spelling words.

Write the spelling words that have the long *o* sound spelled *o*.

1. _____

Write the spelling words that have the long *o* sound spelled *oa*.

2. _____ 3. _____

4. _____

Write the spelling words that have the long *o* sound spelled *ow*.

5. _____ 6. _____

7. _____ 8. _____

Write the spelling words that have the long *o* sound spelled *oe*.

9. _____ 10. _____

B. A letter is missing from each spelling word below. Write the missing letter in the box. Then write the spelling word correctly on the line.

11. fl ⬜ ating _____ 12. kn ⬜ w _____

13. wo ⬜ _____ 14. clo ⬜ k _____

15. mo ⬜ stly _____

Name _____

> • **Past-tense verbs** tell about actions that already happened.
> • To form the past tense of regular verbs, add **-ed** to the present tense of the verb.
>
>   Last month our class <u>cleaned</u> the park.

A. Circle the past-tense verb in each sentence. Write it on the line.

1. Our class picked up trash. _____

2. We looked for litter. _____

3. We also cleaned the playground. _____

4. Tammy raked some leaves. _____

5. Bill and Jen planted flowers. _____

B. Choose two past-tense verbs you circled above. Use them in two new sentences. Write the sentences on the lines.

6. _____

_____

7. _____

_____

 Use the sentences as a model. Write about a trip you went on with your family. Tell where you went and what you did.

Name _____

- A **future-tense verb** tells an action that will happen in the future.
- To form a future-tense verb, add the word *will* before the verb.

  Eric <u>will rake</u> the leaves tomorrow.

A. Write the future tense of the verb to complete each sentence.

1. Ling and Mia _____ at school next week. (help)

2. They _____ in the library. (work)

3. On Monday, they _____ to the younger children. (read)

4. Ling _____ books for children. (find)

5. Mia _____ the books to the children. (show)

6. On Tuesday, they _____ some new books. (sort)

B. Write one future-tense verb from above in a new sentence.

7. _____

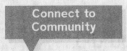
Connect to Community Plan an event for your community. Tell what will happen at the event and how the event will help people in the community. Use future-tense verbs.

Name _____

> • Use a comma after the greeting in a letter. Capitalize all the words in the greeting.
> • Use a comma after the closing in a letter. Capitalize only the first word in the closing.

Rewrite the letter with correct punctuation.

> Dear officer Walker
>
>   Thank you for helping our community. You help everyone stay safe!
>
>   Yours Truly
>   Mr. Neff's class

_____

_____

_____

_____

Name _____

> • Add **-ed** to most verbs to tell about an action in the past.
> • Add the word **will** before a verb to tell about the future.

Draw a line below each mistake in the letter. Then rewrite the paragraph correctly on the lines.

Dear Emma,

Yesterday, our class pick up trash at the park. We plant flowers. Next week, our class visit the police station. Our class learn how to be safe.

Your friend,
Jess

_____

_____

_____

_____

Name _____

A. Rewrite each sentence to tell about the past. Change the verb in ( ) to the past tense.

1. Our class _____ as a team last Saturday. (work)

_____

2. We _____ with Mrs. Johnson. (talk)

_____

3. She _____ us to plant flowers. (want)

_____

B. Rewrite each sentence to tell about the future. Change the underlined verb to the future tense.

4. We <u>get</u> some seeds.

_____

5. We <u>plant</u> the seeds.

_____

6. The flowers <u>make</u> the park a beautiful place.

_____

Writing/Spelling Connection Look back through your writer's notebook for a past-tense verb you used. Check that you used it correctly. Now look for a future-tense verb. Check that you used a future-tense verb correctly.

Name _____

> **Expand your vocabulary by adding or removing inflectional endings, prefixes, or suffixes to a base word to create different forms of a word.**

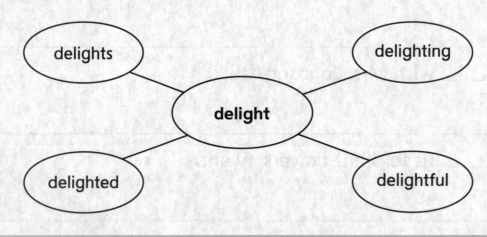

Use your notes from "Starry Night." Choose one word and write it in the word web. Add circles to the web to write as many related words as you can. Use a dictionary to help you.

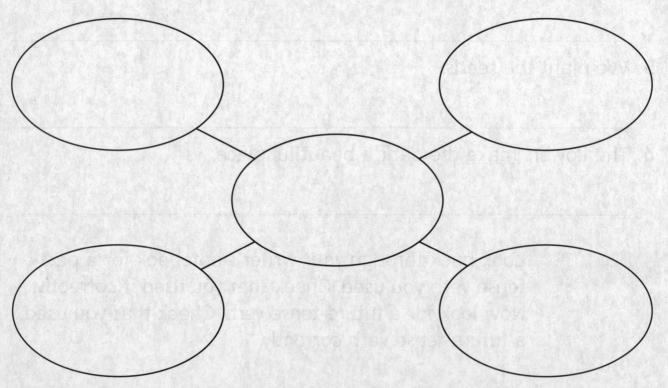

Name _____

Read the clues. Complete the puzzle with your vocabulary words. Use the letters in the boxes to solve the riddle.

across	behave	borrow	countryside
covered	express	solution	villages

1. Land without many people _ _ _ _ _ _ _ _ _ _ ☐ _

2. From one side to the other _ _ _ ☐ _ _

3. To take but then give back _ _ _ _ ☐ _

4. Coated in _ _ _ _ ☐ _ _

5. To act ☐ _ _ _ _ _ _

6. To say or show _ _ _ _ ☐ _ _

7. Small towns _ _ _ ☐ _ _ _ _

8. The way to fix a problem _ _ ☐ _ _ _ _ _

What never asks questions but is always answered?

A ☐ ☐ ☐ ☐ ☐ ☐ ☐ ☐

Name _____

> Every syllable in a word must have a vowel sound.

Say the picture name. Then say the syllables in the word. Draw an X for each syllable you hear. Write the number of syllables on the line.

1.

2.

3.

4.

Teacher Directions: Model 1. *Listen as I say the first word:* hel-met. *Say the syllables with me.* Model drawing 2 X's and writing the number of syllables on the line.

Name _____

Listen to the sounds your teacher says. Blend the sounds to make a word. Circle the picture that goes with that word.

1.

2.

3.

4.

5.

Teacher Directions: Model item 1 by saying: */k/ /w/ /ē/ /n/. Listen as I blend these sounds:* /kwēēēnnn/, queen. *I see a picture that shows a queen so I will circle it.* Guide children to blend the sounds and circle the picture. For items 2-5, have children listen to the sounds, blend them to form a word, and circle the correct picture. 2. /h/ /ī/ /v/; 3. /s/ /t/ /r/ /ē/ /m/; 4. /b/ /l/ /o/ /k/ /s/; 5. /f/ /i/ /sh/.

Name _____

> Some words have a long *e* sound. Listen to the vowel sound in the words *he* and *bee*. The letters *e, ee, ea, ie, y, ey,* or *e_e* can stand for this sound.
>
> | he | bee | leaf | shield | sunny | key | Eve |
> |----|-----|------|--------|-------|-----|-----|
> | | | | | | | |

A. Underline the letters that stand for the long *e* sound in the words below.

be	eat	field	free
green	peas	seeds	complete
eager	even	family	money

B. Choose a word from the list above to fill in each blank. Write the word on the line.

Today, my _____ planted _____ and

_____ beans in a _____. I am

_____ to _____ them. They will _____

a _____ meal that will not cost _____.

_____ the _____ were _____.

Name _____

The Seal

It is time to feed Eve the seal. Eve is hungry for fish. She

leaps up. She gets a piece of fish!

Pete will teach Eve. Each time she completes a feat,

Pete gives her a treat! Pete teaches Eve each day. Repeating

her feats is key. Pete believes in Eve.

Eve is on the seal team. The seals compete in a big

show. Then Pete feeds each seal. Eve gets three treats! The

treats are yummy fish. They mean big money for Eve.

Eve is the lead seal in her field. She is shiny and clean.

She has to be seen! She is indeed the queen. Kids like to see

Eve steal the show!

1. Circle all the words with long *e* sounds.

2. Complete the sentences.

Eve is the lead seal in her _____.

She is _____ and clean.

Name _____

A word that means one of something is called singular: *baby*.

A word that means more than one of something is called plural: *babies*.

Most of the time, we add *-s* to a singular word to make it plural. But if the singular word ends in a consonant followed by a *y*, we change the *y* to *i* and then add *-es*.

A. Next to each singular word, write the plural form of the word on the line.

1. bird _____

2. cub _____

3. family _____

4. friend _____

5. job _____

6. pony _____

7. penny _____

8. plum _____

B. Next to each plural word, write the singular form of the word.

9. babies _____

10. foods _____

11. puppies _____

12. shrubs _____

13. stories _____

14. years _____

Writing/Spelling Connection

Look back through your writer's notebook for plurals you have used. Check that you followed the spelling rules above. Fix any mistakes you find.

Name _____

Complete each sentence. Use the words in the box.

after	before	every	few	first
hear	hurt	old	special	would

1. I am seven years _____.

2. I _____ like to go see you now.

3. Do not eat the candy until _____ dinner.

4. I only had time to draw a _____ pictures.

5. Put on your coat _____ you go out.

6. If this is your _____ time here, let us give you a map.

7. We like this place so much, we come here _____ year.

8. This teddy bear is _____ because it is the one I like best.

9. It is hard to _____ you from so far away.

10. Look where you are walking so you will not fall and get _____.

Name _____

Fold back the paper along the dotted line. Use the blanks to write each word as it is read aloud. When you finish the test, unfold the paper. Use the list at the right to correct any spelling mistakes.

1. _____   1. we

2. _____   2. bee

3. _____   3. need

4. _____   4. queen

5. _____   5. mean

6. _____   6. leaf

7. _____   7. thief

8. _____   8. chief

9. _____   9. pony

10. _____   10. keys

Review Words

11. _____   11. grow

12. _____   12. toe

High-Frequency Words

13. _____   13. after

14. _____   14. every

15. _____   15. special

Name _____

we	bee	need	queen	mean
leaf	thief	chief	pony	keys

A. Look at the spelling words in the box. Match the spelling word with the vowel pattern and write the word.

e   *y*   *ey*

1. _____   2. _____   3. _____

ee   *ea*   *ie*

4. _____   7. _____   9. _____

5. _____   8. _____   10. _____

6. _____

B. Write a spelling word that rhymes with each word below.

11. see _____   12. feed _____

13. bony _____   14. lean _____

15. brief _____

Look back through your writer's notebook for words you used that have long *e* spelling patterns. Check that you spelled them correctly. Fix any mistakes you find.

Name _____

we	bee	need	green	bean
seat	thief	chief	pony	key

A. Look at the spelling words in the box. Match the spelling word with the vowel pattern and write the word.

e

1. _____

y

2. _____

ey

3. _____

ee

4. _____

5. _____

6. _____

ea

7. _____

8. _____

ie

9. _____

10. _____

B. Write a spelling word that rhymes with each word below.

11. see _____

12. feed _____

13. bony _____

14. lean _____

15. brief _____

Writing/Spelling Connection

Look back through your writer's notebook for words you used that have long *e* spelling patterns. Check that you spelled them correctly. Fix any mistakes you find.

Name _____

we've	she's	needed	queen	meaning
leaves	grief	chiefs	fifty	keys

A. Look at the spelling words in the box. Match the spelling word with the vowel pattern and write the word.

e

1. _____

2. _____

y

3. _____

ey

4. _____

ee

5. _____

6. _____

ea

7. _____

8. _____

ie

9. _____

10. _____

B. Write a spelling word that rhymes with each word below.

11. sees _____

12. weeded _____

13. leave _____

14. lean _____

15. brief _____

 Writing/Spelling Connection

Look back through your writer's notebook for words you used that have long *e* spelling patterns. Check that you spelled them correctly. Fix any mistakes you find.

Name _____

The subject and verb in a sentence must match, or agree.
If the subject is one person or thing, it is a singular subject and
the sentence must have a singular verb.

The boy <u>looks</u> at the cat.

The girl <u>walks</u> to the dog.

If the subject is more than one person or thing, it is a plural
subject and the sentence must have a plural verb. Usually, we
make the plural form of the verb by taking away the **-s** from
the end of the singular verb.

The boys <u>look</u> at the cat.

The girls <u>walk</u> the dog.

Write the correct verb on the line to complete each sentence.

1. The dog _____.
   run   runs

2. The dogs _____.
   run   runs

3. The cat _____.
   play   plays

4. The cats _____.
   play   plays

 Write a story about three children. Tell about some things they
do together and some things they do apart. Make sure your
sentences are complete and that the subjects and verbs agree.
Correct any mistakes.

Name _____

When a plural noun or a plural pronoun is the subject of a sentence, the verb should be plural. When a singular noun or a singular pronoun is the subject of a sentence, the verb should be singular.

She <u>eats</u> lunch.   He <u>waits</u> in line.

They <u>eat</u> lunch.   We <u>wait</u> in line.

The subject of a sentence can have more than one noun or pronoun in it. If there is more than one noun or pronoun in the subject of a sentence, the verb should be plural.

The <u>boy</u> eats lunch.   She <u>waits</u> in line.

The <u>boy</u> and girl eat lunch.   He and she <u>wait</u> in line.

Write the correct verb on the line to complete each sentence.

1. They _____ a cake.
        bake   bakes

2. The boy and his dog _____ up the street.
        walk   walks

3. The cat and the dog _____ here.
        sleep   sleeps

4. He and the baby _____ under the tree.
        eat   eats

Connect to Community Think of a group of people in your community. Explain how people in the group work with each other and with others. Make sure your subjects and verbs agree.

Name _____

> • An **abbreviation** is a shortened form of a word. It begins with a capital letter and ends with a period. Street names are often abbreviated.
>
> Street → St.   Avenue → Ave.   Drive → Dr.   Road → Rd.
> • The abbreviation of a **title** before a name begins with a capital letter and ends with a period. First and last names are proper nouns and begin with capital letters.
>
> Dr. Allen   Mrs. Lucas   Ms. Jennifer Bailey

A. Write each name and abbreviation correctly.

1. mr mark adams

2. dr jerry gordon

_____

3. ms amy smith

4. mrs. mary jones

_____

B. Write each address using an abbreviation.

5. 245 Flame Street

6. 563 Cherry Avenue

_____

7. 749 Wilson Drive

8. 322 Valley Road

_____

Name _____

A. Circle the subjects that tell about more than one.

1. My sister and I

2. We

3. Tom

4. He

5. He and I

B. Write the correct verb on the line to complete each sentence.

My sister and I _____ the bus to school.

  ride rides

We _____ home.

  walk walks

Tom _____ with us.

  walk walks

He _____ next door to us.

  live lives

He _____ catch with me at school some days.

  play plays

He and I _____ some of those books.

  like likes

Name _____

The Lake

Dad and I like to ride bikes. We rides around the lake. Dad ride fast. I work hard to catch up with Dad. Dad waits for me. We ride under trees. We go past many houses.

My friends Jane and Jill lives near the lake. They waves to Dad and me when they see us. Jane and Jill comes with us on their bikes some days. Jane stop when we see ducks. Jane loves ducks. We all watch the ducks. Two ducks swims across the lake. One duck sit on the shore.

Dad's friends go to the lake, too. Some days Mr. Smith wave to us from his boat. Mr. Smith takes his boat out on the lake a lot. Some days Mrs. Smith is there too. They talks a while. Jane, Jill, and I talks too. Then Jill skates home. Jane rides her bike home. Dad and I ride home too. Dad smile at me. "We all get to see our friends when we bike around the lake," Dad says.

A. The subject and verb of a sentence should always agree. Circle the verbs that do not agree with their subjects.

B. Write on the lines to finish the sentences. Tell what happens at the lake.

1. Jane and Jill _____.

2. Mr. and Mrs. Smith _____.

3. Dad _____.

Look back through your writer's notebook for a story you wrote. Check that your subjects and verbs agree with each other. Fix any mistakes you find.

Name _____

> A **compound word** is a word made of two smaller words.

A. Read each sentence. Write the compound word. Draw a line between the two smaller words.

1. There was not a cloud anywhere. _____

2. They ran around the campsite. _____

3. They saw lots of big evergreen trees. _____

4. There are fireflies here. _____

B. Write the meaning of each compound word.

5. afternoon

_____

6. daylight

_____

7. everyone

_____

8. nightfall

_____

Name _____

> **Multiple-meaning words** have more than one meaning.
> Use other words in the sentence to figure out which
> meaning is being used.

**Read each sentence. Figure out the meaning of the word in
bold print. Put a checkmark in the box before the meaning
that matches its use in the sentence.**

1. The mother can carry the babies on her **back**.

   ☐ the part of the body opposite the front

   ☐ to move away from something

2. The opossum has a **pointed** snout with a pink nose.

   ☐ having a sharp end

   ☐ showed where something is

3. Soon the young animals are **free** to roam.

   ☐ costing no money

   ☐ not held captive

4. When **rattled** by a predator, they lie still and don't move
   at all until the threat goes away.

   ☐ made upset or disturbed

   ☐ made noise

Name _____

Listen as your teacher reads the directions.

1.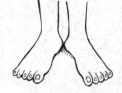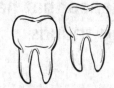

2.

3.

4.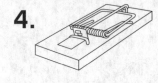

5.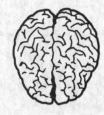

Teacher Directions: Explain to children that we can add sounds to words and take away sounds from words to make new words. Model item 1: *This is a picture of feet. Take away the /f/ sound to make a new word:* eat. *Say the word. Now circle the picture that shows it.* Model item 2: *This is a picture of an ox. Add the sound /b/ to it to make a new word: /b/ /o/ /ks/, box. Say the word, and circle the picture that shows it.* Guide children to complete the rest. 3. *pants*: take away /p/; 4. *trap*: add /s/; 5. *brain*: take away /b/.

Name _____

Alliteration means using many words in a sentence that have the same beginning sounds.

Listen to the sentences and circle the words that complete the sentences using alliteration.

1.

2.

3.

4.

Teacher Directions: Have children look at the picture in the box. Say: *Mike made muffins.* Emphasize /m/ as you say the sentence. Say: *This sentence has alliteration because all of the words begin with the same sound: /m/.* Then read the sentences and have children circle the word that completes it using alliteration: 1. The boy sees a beautiful blue _____. Bird, flower, plane. 2. He can keep the keys in his _____. Coat, shirt, hand. 3. She shall shop for shiny _____. Gloves, socks, shoes. 4. Look at the long line of little _____. Clouds, dolls, leaves.

Name _____

The long *u* sound can be spelled with the letters ***u_e*** or ***ue***, as in the words *cute* and *rescue*.

c<u>u</u>t<u>e</u>   res<u>cue</u>

A. Look at each picture. Write the missing letters to finish the picture name.

1. c ____ b ____

2. am ____ s ____ d

3. f ____ ____ l

4.  conf ____ s ____ d

5.  h ____ g ____

6. 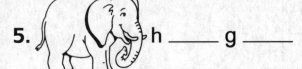 m ____ l ____

B. Use three of the words above to fill in the blanks and complete the sentences below.

1. She rode a _____ up the trail.

2. We stopped to buy _____.

3. I laugh when I am _____.

Name _____

> The long *u* sound can be spelled with the letters *u_e*, *ew*, *ue*, or
> *u* as in the words *cube*, *few*, *music*, and *cue*.
>
> c<u>u</u>b<u>e</u>   m<u>u</u>sic

**A. Underline the letters that stand for the long *u* sound in the
words below.**

music	skew	rescue	mute
refuse	value	unit	spew

B. Circle each word from above in the puzzle below.

i	x	a	y	r	d	g	o
v	a	l	u	e	b	f	y
w	o	s	t	s	p	e	w
m	u	s	i	c	z	s	b
u	s	k	i	u	n	i	t
t	k	e	j	e	h	m	n
e	x	w	r	y	k	p	n
q	r	e	f	u	s	e	h

Name _____

> Add the ending **-er** to a word to compare two things. Add
> the ending **-est** to a word to compare three or more things.
>
> Pine Street is <u>long**er**</u> than Oak Street. add **-er** to **long**
> High Street is the <u>long**est**</u> street of all. add **-est** to **long**

**A. Add *-er* and *-est* to each word to make new words.
Write the words on the lines.**

	Add *-er*	**Add *-est***
1. kind	_____	_____
2. strong	_____	_____
3. cheap	_____	_____
4. pink	_____	_____
5. tight	_____	_____

**B. Write the correct form of the word in parentheses ( ) to
complete each sentence.**

6. My desk is (clean) _____ than Nate's desk.

7. That is the (deep) _____ lake in the state.

8. James is (old) _____ than me.

Name _____

Complete each sentence. Use the words in the box.

America	beautiful	began	climbed	come
country	didn't	give	live	turned

1. He _____ around to look at you.

2. She _____ to the top of the tall tree.

3. We wanted to _____ in this valley.

4. I live in the United States of _____.

5. The girls always _____ back before dark.

6. This picture shows how _____ the lake was.

7. They _____ know the story until I told them.

8. I fell down, but I got up and _____ running again.

9. Would you _____ me a pen so I can write this down?

10. My mom came to this _____ on a plane.

Name _____

Fold back the paper
along the dotted line.
Use the blanks to write
each word as it is read
aloud. When you finish
the test, unfold the
paper. Use the list at
the right to correct
any spelling mistakes.

1. _____

2. _____

3. _____

4. _____

5. _____

6. _____

7. _____

8. _____

9. _____

10. _____

Review Words   11. _____

12. _____

**High-Frequency
Words**   13. _____

14. _____

15. _____

1. cube

2. fumes

3. huge

4. music

5. unit

6. menu

7. few

8. pew

9. fuel

10. cues

11. pony

12. queen

13. began

14. come

15. give

Name _____

> | cube | fumes | huge | music | unit |
> | menu | few | pew | fuel | cues |

A. Look at the spelling words in the box. Match the spelling word with the vowel pattern and write the word.

u_e

1. _____

2. _____

3. _____

u

4. _____

5. _____

6. _____

ew

7. _____

8. _____

ue

9. _____

10. _____

B. An extra letter has been added to each spelling word below. Draw a line through the letter that does not belong. Write the correct word on the line.

11. menue _____

12. huege _____

13. uenit _____

14. muesic _____

15. fuemes _____

Name _____

| cube | fumes | huge | music | unit |
| menu | few | pew | fuel | cue |

A. Look at the spelling words in the box. Match the spelling word with the vowel pattern and write the word.

u_e

1. _____

2. _____

3. _____

u

4. _____

5. _____

6. _____

ew

7. _____

8. _____

ue

9. _____

10. _____

B. An extra letter has been added to each spelling word below. Draw a line through the letter that does not belong. Write the correct word on the line.

11. menue _____

12. huege _____

13. uenit _____

14. muesic _____

15. fuemes _____

Name _____

huge	using	cues	humid	units
menus	few	pews	rescue	continue

A. Look at the spelling words in the box. Match the spelling word with the vowel pattern and write the word.

ue

1. _____

2. _____

3. _____

u

4. _____

5. _____

6. _____

7. _____

ew

8. _____

9. _____

u_e

10. _____

B. An extra letter has been added to each spelling word below. Draw a line through the letter that does not belong. Write the correct word on the line.

11. menues _____

13. uenits _____

15. puews _____

12. huege _____

14. huemid _____

Name _____

> • The verb *have* has two forms in the present tense.
> • Use *has* when the subject is singular.
>   Our class <u>has</u> a weather station.
> • When the subject is plural or *I* or *you,* use the form *have*.
>   Marta and Joe <u>have</u> boots.
>   I <u>have</u> my umbrella.
>   You <u>have</u> a scarf.

A. Complete each sentence with *has* or *have.*

1. I _____ new boots.

2. Matt _____ a raincoat.

3. Lily and Jack _____ warm mittens.

4. You _____ an umbrella.

5. Sara _____ gloves.

B. Write one sentence with *has* and one with *have.*

6. _____

7. _____

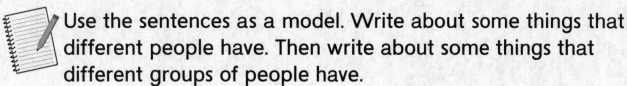 Use the sentences as a model. Write about some things that different people have. Then write about some things that different groups of people have.

Name _____

> • The past tense of **have** is **had**.
> • Use **had** with a singular or plural subject.
>   I <u>had</u> a yellow raincoat.
>   We <u>had</u> a bad storm last night.

Use the word *had* to complete each sentence. Write the new sentence on the line.

1. I _____ a book about storms.

   _____

2. We _____ a plan for bad weather.

   _____

3. Jim _____ a raincoat.

   _____

4. Rick and Dan _____ an umbrella.

   _____

Connect to Community   Explain some things you, your family, or your friends have that can be used to help others in your community.

Name _____

> • Begin every sentence with a capital letter.
> • A period ends a statement and a command.
> • A question mark ends a question.
> • An exclamation point ends an exclamation.
>> This is today's song.
>> Please play this music.
>> Can you play this?
>> This music is hard!

Read the sentences. Write the sentences correctly on the lines.

1. please come to my concert

_____

2. this is an awesome song

_____

3. let's begin playing now.

_____

4. does anyone want to dance

_____

Name _____

> - The verb *have* has two forms in the present tense: *have* and *has*.
> - Use *has* when the subject is singular. Use *have* when the subject is plural or *I* or *you*.
> - The past-tense form of *have* is *had*. Use it with any subject.

Correct the mistakes in the paragraph. Rewrite it correctly on the lines provided.

    Our teacher reads us a book called <u>Watching the Weather</u>. It have lots of facts about weather. Last week, we has a weather forecaster talk to us. She have many stories about storms. Now, we has to tell our own storm stories. Do you had stories? Last week we have a storm here that knocked down a tree in my family's yard.

_____

_____

_____

_____

_____

Name _____

Circle the correct form of the verb *have*.

1. My friend Kim and I (have, has) a weather station.

2. Kim (have, has) it set up in her yard.

3. It (have, has) a thermometer and wind vane.

4. Last week, we (have, had) the thermometer at school.

5. Yesterday, the thermometer (have, had) a temperature of 90°!

6. I (has, have) never seen it that high!

7. We (have, has) records of the weather.

8. The records (have, has) temperatures from last winter.

Look back through your writer's notebook for places you used the verb *have*. Check that you used it correctly. Fix any mistakes you find.

Name _____

> To figure out the meaning of a word, look for a **prefix**, or word part, at the beginning of the word.
>
> The prefix *re-* means "again."
>
> The prefix *dis-* means "opposite of."
>
> The prefix *un-* means "not."

A. Read each sentence. Underline the word that has a prefix. Then write the word and its meaning.

1. We will review what we have talked about.

_____

2. We disagree about what to do next.

_____

3. I like this book so much that I often reread it.

_____

4. Sam was unhappy about getting sick.

_____

B. Write a sentence using each word.

5. dislike _____

6. rewrite _____

7. undo _____

Name _____

Read the clues. Complete the puzzle with your vocabulary words. Use the letters in the boxes to solve the riddle.

adventure	delighted	enjoyed	flapping
idea	lonely	neighbor	nighttime

1. A thought __ __ ☐ __

2. Had fun __ ☐ __ __ __ __ __

3. A fun new thing to do __ __ ☐ __ __ __ __ __ __ __

4. When the sky is dark __ __ __ __ __ __ __ __ ☐ __

5. Feeling alone __ __ __ __ ☐ __

6. A person who lives nearby __ __ __ __ __ __ ☐ __

7. Moving wings up and down __ __ __ __ ☐ __ __ __

8. Made happy __ __ __ __ __ __ __ ☐ __

What word begins and ends with an E but has only one letter?

Name _____

Say the name of each picture. Say the middle sound in both words. Draw a line to the picture on the right whose name has the same middle sound.

1.

2.

3.

4.

5.

6.

Teacher Directions: Model item 1. *Bike. Five. The middle sound of these words is /ī/. Let me find the word on the right that has the /ī/ sound.* Say the picture names. Kite *has the /ī/ sound in the middle too.* Have children complete the rest of the items.

Name _____

Say each picture name. Listen to the middle sound. Place an X on the picture with a different middle sound.

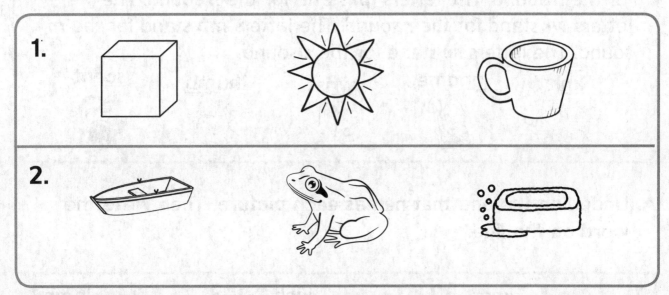

Say each picture name. Figure out if the vowel sound in the first syllable is long or short. Place an X on the picture with the vowel sound that is different.

Teacher Directions: 3 Model Say *beagle, petal, people* stressing the vowel sound in the first syllable. Beagle *and* people *have the /ē/ sound. Petal has the /e/ sound. It is different.* Guide children to place an X on the word. Have children complete #4.

Name _____

Some consonant pairs have a silent letter. The letters **kn** stand for the **n** sound. The letters **gn** stand for the **n** sound. The letters **wr** stand for the **r** sound. The letters **mb** stand for the **m** sound. The letters **sc** stand for the **s** sound.

knit   **g**nome   **w**rist   thu**mb**   **sc**ent

A. Underline the one that names each picture. Then write the word on the line.

1.	knot not know	2.	inch wrench wrist	3.	lamp limb lamb
____		____		____	
4.	scent scene scissors	5.	knife knee night	6.	gap gnat nap
____		____		____	

B. In the words you underlined above, circle the letter pair that includes a silent consonant.

Name _____

Some consonant pairs have a silent letter. The letters **kn** stand for the **n** sound. The letters **gn** stand for the **n** sound. The letters **wr** stand for the **r** sound. The letters **mb** stand for the **m** sound. The letters **sc** stand for the **s** sound.

<u>kn</u>ee	<u>gn</u>at	<u>wr</u>ench	la<u>mb</u>	<u>sc</u>ene

Look at each picture. Write the missing letters to finish spelling the picture name.

wr	kn	gn	mb	sc

1. _____ ight	**2.** _____ ite
3. thu _____	**4.** desi _____
5. _____ ientist	**6.** _____ ot
7. _____ ome	**8.** co _____

Name _____

A **prefix** is a word part added to the beginning of a word to change its meaning. A **suffix** is a word part added to the end of a word to change its meaning.

The prefix *un-* means "not."

The prefix *re-* means "again."

The prefix *dis-* means "opposite of."

The suffix *-ful* means "full of."

The suffix *-less* means "without."

A. Match each sentence to a word with a prefix or suffix. Use the underlined words to help you.

1. Her shoes are <u>not</u> <u>tied</u>.   **a.** retold

2. He is going <u>without</u> a <u>tie</u>.   **b.** tieless

3. They <u>told</u> that story <u>again</u>.   **c.** untied

4. This story has <u>not</u> been <u>told</u>.   **d.** untold

B. Read the words. Circle the best meaning for each word.

5. cheerful	full of cheer	without cheer
6. disobey	obey again	opposite of obey
7. leafless	full of leaves	without leaves
8. rewrite	write again	opposite of write
9. unsigned	signed again	not signed

Name _____

Complete each sentence. Use the words in the box.

below	colors	don't	down	eat
many	morning	sleep	through	very

1. He has been _____ helpful to me.

2. Dad and I hiked _____ the tunnel.

3. Her dress has all the _____ of a rainbow.

4. I am glad we have so _____ good friends.

5. The plates are on the shelf _____ the bowls.

6. You should _____ for eight hours every night.

7. Mom gets up very early every _____ for work.

8. He walked _____ the steps to the swimming pool.

9. I am so hungry that I can hardly wait to _____ lunch.

10. I like all of those foods, so I _____ care which is for dinner.

Name _____

Fold back the paper along the dotted line. Use the blanks to write each word as it is read aloud. When you finish the test, unfold the paper. Use the list at the right to correct any spelling mistakes.

1. _____
2. _____
3. _____
4. _____
5. _____
6. _____
7. _____
8. _____
9. _____
10. _____

Review Words

11. _____
12. _____

High-Frequency Words

13. _____
14. _____
15. _____

1. comb
2. crumb
3. scene
4. scent
5. gnat
6. sign
7. knife
8. know
9. wrist
10. writing
11. first
12. music
13. very
14. eat
15. don't

Name _____

comb	crumb	scene	scent	gnat
sign	knife	know	wrist	writing

A. Write the words that have each silent letter pair.

wr

1. _____

2. _____

gn

5. _____

6. _____

sc

9. _____

10. _____

kn

3. _____

4. _____

mb

7. _____

8. _____

B. Write the missing letter in the box. Then write the spelling word correctly on the line.

11. ☐nife _____

13. si☐n _____

15. ☐rist _____

12. com☐ _____

14. s☐ene _____

Name _____

| lamb | thumb | scene | scent | gnat |
| sign | knife | know | wrap | write |

A. Write the words that have each silent letter pair.

wr

1. _____

2. _____

gn

5. _____

6. _____

sc

9. _____

10. _____

kn

3. _____

4. _____

mb

7. _____

8. _____

B. Write the missing letter in the box. Then write the spelling word correctly on the line.

11. ☐nife _____

12. lam☐_____

13. si☐n _____

14. s☐ene _____

15. ☐rap _____

Name _____

combed	crumbs	scenes	scents	gnats
signed	knife	known	wrists	writing

A. Write the words that have each silent letter pair.

wr

1. _____

2. _____

gn

5. _____

6. _____

sc

9. _____

10. _____

kn

3. _____

4. _____

mb

7. _____

8. _____

B. Write the missing letter in the box. Then write the spelling word correctly on the line.

11. ☐nife _____

12. com☐ed _____

13. si☐ned _____

14. s☐enes _____

15. ☐rists _____

Name _____

- A **linking verb** connects the subject to the rest of the sentence.
- A linking verb does not show action.
- The linking verb *be* has special forms in the present tense: *is*, *are*, and *am*.

    Parrots <u>are</u> birds.

    The forest <u>is</u> big.

    I <u>am</u> in the forest.

A. Circle the linking verb in each sentence.

1. Forests are busy places.

2. I am near a large tree.

3. A bird is in the tree.

4. A snake is near the bird.

5. Other animals are in the tree, too.

B. Write a sentence of your own using a linking verb.

6.  .

 Use the sentences as a model. Write about who you are and who else is important in your life. Use linking verbs to tell about yourself and the people who matter most to you.

Name _____

> • A **linking verb** does not show action. Linking verbs can show ideas from the past.
> • The past-tense forms of the linking verb *be* include ***was*** (singular) and ***were*** (plural).
>   I <u>am</u> in Africa. Last week, I <u>was</u> in New York.
>   The lion <u>is</u> in the tree. Earlier, it <u>was</u> in the grass.
>   We <u>are</u> awake. Last night, we <u>were</u> asleep.

Choose the correct linking verb in ( ). Write the complete sentence.

1. Last week, I (was, were) near the ocean.

_____

2. There (was, were) whales nearby.

_____

3. The birds (was, were) in the sky.

_____

4. Boats (was, were) in the distance.

_____

5. The scene (was, were) peaceful.

_____

Name _____

> • All the words in a letter's **greeting** begin with a capital letter.
> • Only the first word in the **closing** of a letter begins with a capital letter.
> • Use a **comma** after the greeting and closing of a friendly letter.

Rewrite the letter correctly.

dear mark

   I like learning about nature. What do you like to learn about?

                         your friend
                         Lizzie

_____

_____

_____

_____

Name _____

> • A **linking verb** does not show action.
> • The **present-tense** forms of the linking verb *be* are *is, am*, and *are*.
> • The **past-tense** forms of the linking verb *be* are *was* and *were*.

Read the paragraph and underline the mistakes. Then rewrite the paragraph correctly on the lines.

A rain forest are a wonderful place. There is rain forests in the United States. The largest one are in Alaska. It are called Tongass National Forest. Other rain forests is in Washington. Was you ever in a rain forest?

_____

_____

_____

_____

Connect to Community Write about the community where you live. What is it like? Tell how it is different from some other communities. Use linking verbs as you write.

Name _____

Circle the present-tense form of the linking verb *be* in each sentence. Rewrite the sentence. Change the verb to the past tense.

1. I am in the grasslands.

_____

2. Zebras are nearby.

_____

3. The grass is brown.

_____

4. Animals are in the grass.

_____

5. We are near the water hole.

_____

6. Food for the animals is all around us.

_____

Look back through your writer's notebook for linking verbs you have used. Check that you used them correctly. Fix any mistakes you find.

Name _____

Expand your vocabulary by adding or removing inflectional endings, prefixes, or suffixes to or from a base word to create different forms of a word.

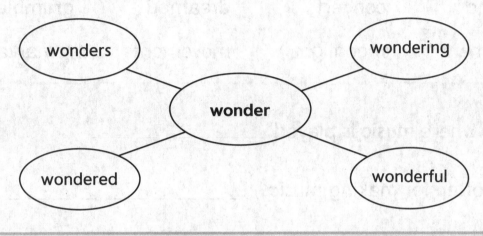

Use your notes from "Happy New Year!" Choose one word and write it in the word web. Add circles to the web to write as many related words as you can. Use a dictionary to help you.

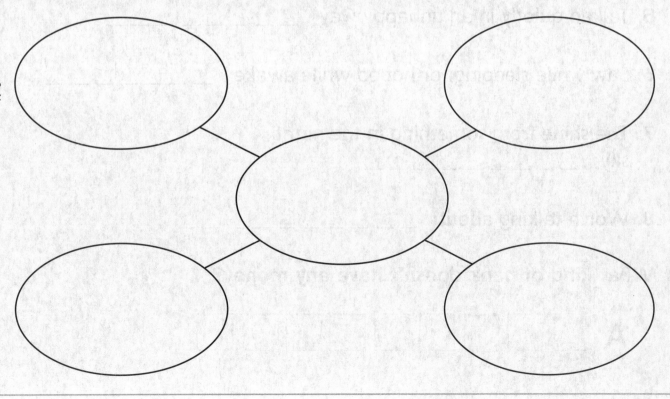

Name _____

Read the clues. Complete the puzzle with the vocabulary words below. Use the letters in the boxes to solve the riddle.

cheered	concert	dreamed	grumbled
instrument	moonlight	movements	remarkable

1. A show where music is played _ _ _ _ _☐_

2. A tool, often for making music ☐_ _ _ _ _ _ _ _ _ _

3. Acts such as stepping or turning _ _ ☐_ _ ☐_ _ _

4. Clapped at the end of a good show _ _ _ _ ☐_ _ _

5. Talked quietly in an unhappy way _ _ _ _ ☐_ _ _

6. Saw while sleeping, or hoped while awake _ _ _ ☐_ _ _

7. The shine from something in the night sky _ _ _ ☐_ _ _ _ _

8. Worth talking about _ _ _ _ _ ☐_ _ _

What kind of bank doesn't have any money?

A ☐ ☐ ☐ ☐ ☐ ☐ ☐ ☐ ☐

Name _____

Listen to the sounds your teacher says. Blend the sounds to make a word. Circle the picture that goes with the word.

Teacher Directions: Model item 1 by saying: */b/ /ûr/ /d/. Listen as I blend these sounds: /bûrd/, bird. I see a picture of a bird, so I will circle it.* Guide children to blend the sounds to say the word and circle the picture. For items 2-5, have children listen to the sounds, blend them to say each word, and circle the correct picture. 2. Say: /k/ /ûr/ /l/. 3. Say: /sh/ /r/ /i/ /m/ /p/ 4. Say: /s/ /t/ /u/ /m/ /p/.

Name _____

Listen to the word your teacher says. Change the sound at the end to the new sound your teacher says. Circle the picture of the new word.

1.

2.

3.

4.

5.

Teacher Directions: 1. Model Point to the picture and say: *This is curl. I can change the /l/ sound at the end to a /b/ to make a new word. The new word is curb.* Guide children to say the word and circle the picture. Have them do the following. **2.** *herd;* change /d/ to /t/. **3.** *work;* change /k/ to /m/ **4.** *streak:* change /k/ to /m/ **5.** *wind;* change /d/ to /k/

Name _____

When the letters ***er, ir, or***, or ***ur*** work together, they stand for the sounds you hear in *fern, dirt, world*, and *curl*. It is an *r*-controlled vowel sound.

f<u>er</u>n   d<u>ir</u>t   w<u>or</u>ld   c<u>ur</u>l

A. Underline the letters in each word that stand for the same *r*-controlled vowel sound you hear in the word *shirt*.

verb   turtle   workshop   bird

B. Fill in the blank with the word that has the same *r*-controlled vowel sound as the word *dirt*.

1. It is a _____ day for a picnic.

   a. perfect   **b.** perfume

2. I fell and _____ my knee.

   a. hit   **b.** hurt

3. We hold hands to form a _____ .

   a. certain   **b.** circle

4. My mom and dad _____ in that store.

   a. shop   **b.** work

Name _____

When the letters **er**, **ir**, **or**, or **ur** work together, they stand for the sounds you hear in *herd*, *shirt*, *worm*, and *purse*. It is an *r*-controlled vowel sound.

herd   **shirt**   **worm**   **purse**

Look at each picture. Circle the word that names the picture. Write the word.

1.  _____

   burn   bun

4.  _____

   brother   burger

2.  _____

   giraffe   gerbil

5. _____

   work   woke

3. _____

   perch   peach

6.  _____

   stop   stir

Name _____

> When we add the ending **-ed** or **-ing** to an action word that ends in a single consonant, we double the final consonant.
>
> When we add the ending **-ed** or **-ing** to an action word that ends in a silent **e**, we drop the silent **e**.
>
> When we add the ending **-es** or **-ed** to an action word that ends in a consonant followed by **y**, we change the **y** to **i**.
>
> hum ⟶ hums, hummed, humming
> hike ⟶ hikes, hiked, hiking
> try ⟶ tries, tried, trying

A. Write the word that completes each sentence.

1. The leaves are _____ color.

changeing   changing

2. My dog has _____ his bed.

shreded   shredded

3. Jeff _____ the dishes.

dries   drys

B. Fill in the missing parts to make the word.

4. __bulge_____ - ____e____ + ____ing____ = bulging

5. _____ - _____ + _____ = hurries

6. _____ + _____ + _____ = clapped

Writing/Spelling Connection

Look back through your writer's notebook for words you used that have the endings *-s, -es, -ed,* or *-ing.* Check that you followed the spelling rules above. Fix any mistakes you find.

Name _____

Complete each sentence. Use the words in the box.

animal	away	building	found	from
Saturday	thought	today	toward	watch

1. Cats are my favorite _____.

2. This box was a gift _____ my dad.

3. We went to see Grandpa last _____.

4. We want to _____ a show about dogs.

5. She _____ a penny on the table over there.

6. The _____ where my mom works is very tall.

7. They are going to play catch after school _____.

8. We went _____ from home for a week this summer.

9. He _____ she was late, but he was wrong about what time it was.

10. If you walk _____ school from here, you will get to my house after two blocks.

Name _____

Fold back the paper along the dotted line. Use the blanks to write each word as it is read aloud. When you finish the test, unfold the paper. Use the list at the right to correct any spelling mistakes.

1. _____   1. clerk

2. _____   2. herd

3. _____   3. first

4. _____   4. skirt

5. _____   5. stir

6. _____   6. churn

7. _____   7. hurt

8. _____   8. burst

9. _____   9. work

10. _____   10. worse

Review Words   11. _____   11. know

12. _____   12. wrist

High-Frequency Words   13. _____   13. found

14. _____   14. from

15. _____   15. today

Name _____

clerk	herd	first	skirt	stir
churn	hurt	burst	work	worse

A. Look at the spelling words in the box. Match the spelling word with the *r*-controlled vowel spelling pattern and write the word.

er

1. _____

2. _____

or

3. _____

4. _____

ir

5. _____

6. _____

7. _____

ur

8. _____

9. _____

10. _____

B. Write the missing letter in the box. Then write the spelling word correctly on the line.

11. f☐rst _____

12. b☐rst _____

13. w☐rk _____

14. sk☐rt _____

15. h☐rd _____

Name _____

| her | herd | first | bird | girl |
| turn | hurt | burn | work | worse |

A. Look at the spelling words in the box. Match the spelling word with the *r*-controlled vowel spelling pattern and write the word.

er

1. _____

2. _____

or

3. _____

4. _____

ir

5. _____

6. _____

7. _____

ur

8. _____

9. _____

10. _____

B. Write the missing letter in the box. Then write the spelling word correctly on the line.

11. f☐rst _____

12. b☐rn _____

13. w☐rk _____

14. b☐rd _____

15. h☐rd _____

Name _____

enter	over	thirst	dirty	shirts
churning	nurse	burst	working	worst

A. Look at the spelling words in the box. Match the spelling word with the *r*-controlled vowel spelling pattern and write the word.

er

1. _____

2. _____

or

3. _____

4. _____

ir

5. _____

6. _____

7. _____

ur

8. _____

9. _____

10. _____

B. Write the missing letter in the box. Then write the spelling word correctly on the line.

11. th☐rst _____

12. b☐rst _____

13. w☐rking _____

14. d☐rty _____

15. ent☐r _____

Name _____

- A **helping verb** helps the main verb show action.
- Use *have*, *has*, and *had* to help main verbs show an action in the past.
- Use *has* when the subject is singular. Use *have* or *had* when the subject is plural or *I* or *you*.

  I <u>have</u> seen a wildfire.

  Jack <u>has</u> been to the fire station.

  We <u>had</u> heard the sirens before we saw the fire trucks.

A. Read each sentence. Circle the main verb. Then underline the helping verb.

1. I have read about Earth changes in class.

2. Sometimes weather has caused the changes.

3. Wind has blown sand away.

4. Storms have washed away the soil.

5. I had learned a lot about Earth changes before class ended.

B. Write a sentence of your own using a helping verb.

6. _____

 What would you like to do that you have never done? Do you know people who have done those things? Use helping verbs to write about the things you would like to do and who has done those things.

Name _____

> - A **helping verb** helps the main verb show action.
> - Present-tense helping verbs are *is, am,* and *are*.
> - Use the helping verbs *was* and *were* for the past tense.
>   Rain <u>is</u> pounding on the roof.
>   Jake and Paul <u>were</u> swimming in the ocean.

Circle the correct helping verb in ( ). Write the sentence.

1. I (am, are) learning how water breaks rocks.

_____

2. Rain clouds (was, were) blowing across the sky.

_____

3. Cold air (was, are) freezing the clouds.

_____

4. Now, icy rain (is, are) falling on rocks.

_____

5. Ice (is, were) freezing in the cracks of the rocks.

_____

Name _____

> • Capitalize the first word, the last word, and any important words in book titles.
> • Underline all the words in the title of a book.
>
> I read <u>Holidays for Children</u> last night.
>
> Our teacher told us <u>Dance of the Lion</u> was a good book.

Correct the book titles in the sentences. Write the titles correctly on the lines below.

1. Charlie is reading a book called <u>children near and far</u>.

_____

2. <u>Holidays and festivals for every month</u> is a good book.

_____

3. I like the pictures in a book titled <u>my favorite games</u>.

_____

4. <u>Customs from everywhere</u> is the title of a useful book.

_____

5. To learn different games, read <u>how children play in other places</u>.

_____

Name _____

- The helping verbs *have*, *has*, *had*, *was*, and *were* help the main verb show action that happened in the past.
- The helping verbs *am*, *is*, and *are* help the main verb show action that happens in the present.

Read the paragraph and circle the mistakes. Rewrite the passage correctly on the lines below.

   We is learning about Earth in school. Our teacher said, "Earth changes every day." We has watched a movie about the ocean. Every day, ocean waves is washing away the shore. Now I are excited to learn more about how Earth am changing.

_____

_____

_____

_____

_____

Connect to Community

Write about some interesting things that people in your community have done. Use helping verbs correctly in your writing.

Name _____

Mark the correct helping verb to complete each sentence. Then write the word on the line.

1. The fire _____ burning in the forest.
   ○ are   ○ has
   ○ is   ○ am

2. Firefighters _____ working to put it out.
   ○ has   ○ are
   ○ is   ○ am

3. Animals _____ hiding in the forest.
   ○ are   ○ am
   ○ is   ○ has

4. A firefighter _____ talked to our class last year.
   ○ are   ○ had
   ○ is   ○ am

5. She _____ helped fight many fires.
   ○ were   ○ are
   ○ have   ○ has

6. We _____ listening to her.
   ○ had   ○ has
   ○ were   ○ is

Writing/Spelling Connection — **Look back through your writer's notebook for helping verbs you have used. Check that you used them correctly. Fix any mistakes you find.**

Name _____

A **simile** compares two unlike things. It uses the word *like* or *as* to make the comparison.

Read the sentences. Then answer the questions.

1. Riding a roller coaster can feel like flying.

What two things does the author compare?

_____

What does the simile mean?

_____

_____

2. A motor moves this chain in a loop. It is like the moving belt at the store checkout.

What two things does the author compare?

_____

What does the simile mean?

_____

3. The roller coaster's sound is as loud as thunder.

What two things does the author compare?

_____

What does the simile mean?

_____

Name _____

> The ending **-er** is added to an adjective to compare two nouns. The ending **-est** is added to an adjective to compare more than two nouns. Make these spelling changes when adding either ending:
> - words ending in **y**: change **y** to **i**
> - words with final **e**: drop the final **e**
> - words ending with a vowel and a consonant: double the final consonant

Underline the suffix in the word in bold print. Write the word and its meaning. Then write your own sentence using the word.

1. Socks is the **cutest** cat in the world.

_____

_____

2. He is **happier** than most cats.

_____

_____

3. He is the **biggest** cat on the block.

_____

_____

4. He is **smaller** than my dog.

_____

_____

Name _____

Words that rhyme end with the same sounds.

Say the name of each picture. Then draw two pictures whose names rhyme with it.

1.	
2.	
3.	
4.	

Teacher Directions: Read the box at the top of the page. Point to the pictures as you name each one: *cat, hat, acrobat.* Explain that these words rhyme. Read the directions with children.

Name _____

Listen to the word your teacher says. Change the sound at the end with the new sound your teacher says. Circle the picture of the new word.

Teacher Directions: 1. Model Point to the picture and say: *This is a* plane. *I can change the sound at the end to /t/ to make a new word. The new word is* plate. Guide children to say the word and circle the picture. Have them do the following: 2. *braid;* change /d/ to /n/ 3. *cage;* change /j/ to /k/ 4. *bus;* change /s/ to /g/ 5. *street;* change /t/ to /m/.

Name _____

The letters *or, ore*, and *oar* can stand for the r-controlled vowel sound you hear in *cork, board*, and *store*. The letters *ar* can stand for the r-controlled vowel sound you hear in *star*.

cork

board

store

star

Read the words. Circle the one that names each picture.

1. acorn / artist / adore	**2.** sore / snore / score	**3.** cord / cork / curb
4. starfish / startle / storms	**5.** core / card / chore	**6.** scar / soar / sport

Name _____

The letters *or*, *ore*, and *oar* can stand for the r-controlled vowel sound you hear in *stork*, *roar*, and *snore*. The letters *ar* can stand for the r-controlled vowel sound you hear in *jar*.

st<u>or</u>k   r<u>oar</u>   sn<u>ore</u>   j<u>ar</u>

A. Write *or*, *oar*, *ore*, or *ar* to complete each picture name.

1.  c _____

2.  b _____

3.  h _____ net

4. c _____

B. Finish each word ladder. Change one letter at a time.

5. Go from **corn** to **fork**.

6. Go from **part** to **bark**.

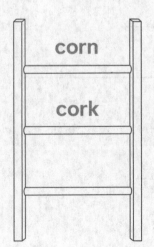

corn

cork

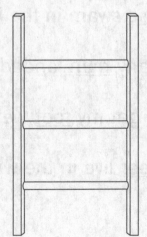

Name _____

> A *plural* noun names more than one. To change a singular
> noun to plural, we usually add *-s* or *-es*.
>
>
>
> rug   rugs   box   boxes
>
>
>
> Some nouns change their spelling to become plural.
>
>
>
> man   men   child   children
>
>
>
> Some nouns do not change their spelling to become plural.
>
>
>
> sheep   sheep
>
>

A. Read the words. Then write the plural form of the word on the line.

1.   child _____   2.   woman _____

3.   mouse _____   4.   tooth _____

B. Read the sentence. Make the underlined word plural.

5.   Six <u>goose</u> swam in the lake. _____

6.   How many <u>man</u> landed on the moon? _____

7.   I like to get my <u>foot</u> wet. _____

8.   Most <u>deer</u> live in the wild. _____

Name _____

Complete each sentence. Use the words in the box.

ago	carry	certain	everyone	heavy
outside	people	problem	together	warm

1. I am _____ I can win this game.

2. We should go _____ to play catch.

3. This box is too _____ for me to lift.

4. We went swimming two days _____.

5. The game helped _____ have a good time.

6. I can _____ your bag if it weighs too much for you.

7. In the winter, you should wear a coat to stay _____.

8. My friends and I all walked home from school _____.

9. My desk shakes because there is a _____ with one of its legs.

10. Most of the _____ from my school are still eating lunch right now.

Name _____

Fold back the paper along the dotted line. Use the blanks to write each word as it is read aloud. When you finish the test, unfold the paper. Use the list at the right to correct any spelling mistakes.

1. _____   1. port

2. _____   2. north

3. _____   3. more

4. _____   4. store

5. _____   5. oar

6. _____   6. roar

7. _____   7. board

8. _____   8. part

9. _____   9. start

10. _____   10. park

Review Words   11. _____   11. first

12. _____   12. hurt

High-Frequency Words   13. _____   13. ago

14. _____   14. carry

15. _____   15. people

Name _____

port	north	more	store	oar
roar	board	part	start	park

A. Look at the spelling words in the box. Match the spelling word with the vowel spelling pattern and write the word.

or

1. _____

2. _____

ore

3. _____

4. _____

oar

5. _____

6. _____

7. _____

ar

8. _____

9. _____

10. _____

B. Write a spelling word that rhymes with each of these words.

11. shark _____

12. sort _____

13. cart _____

14. forth _____

15. hoard _____

Name _____

horn	sort	more	store	oar
roar	board	art	start	car

A. Look at the spelling words in the box. Match the spelling word with the *r*-controlled vowel spelling pattern and write the word.

or

1. _____

2. _____

ore

3. _____

4. _____

oar

5. _____

6. _____

7. _____

ar

8. _____

9. _____

10. _____

B. Write a spelling word that rhymes with each of these words.

11. tar _____

12. born _____

13. cart _____

14. shore _____

15. hoard _____

Name _____

| fork | north | boredom | core | soared |
| roaring | board | spark | parked | charm |

A. Look at the spelling words in the box. Match the spelling word with the *r*-controlled vowel spelling pattern and write the word.

or

1. _____

2. _____

ore

3. _____

4. _____

oar

5. _____

6. _____

7. _____

ar

8. _____

9. _____

10. _____

B. Write a spelling word that rhymes with each of these words.

11. shark _____

12. cork _____

13. harm _____

14. forth _____

15. hoard _____

Name _____

- Some verbs do not add **-ed** to form the past tense.
- These verbs are called **irregular verbs.**
- The verbs **go** and **do** have special forms in the past tense.

  I, he, she, it, we, you, they   go ➞ <u>went</u>

  I, he, she, it, we, you, they   do ➞ <u>did</u>

Rewrite the sentences using the past-tense of the verb in ( ).

1. Our teacher _____ to China. (go)

_____

2. She _____ many interesting things in China. (do)

_____

3. She _____ a lion dance. (do)

_____

4. Our class _____ outside to learn the lion dance. (go)

_____

5. We _____ the dance yesterday for other classes. (do).

_____

 Use the sentences as a model. Write about a trip you have gone on that you liked. Tell where you went and what you did there.

Name _____

> - Irregular verbs do not add **-ed** to form the past tense.
> - The irregular verbs **_see_**, **_say_**, and **_tell_** have special forms in the past tense.
>
>   We <u>saw</u> the fireworks last night.
>   Dad <u>said</u>, "The celebration was the best."
>   He <u>told</u> us that we could go next year.

Rewrite the sentences. Use the past tense of the verb in bold.

1. I **see** some fireworks.

_____

2. I **say**, "Wow! What bright lights!"

_____

3. "Let's come back next year," we **say**.

_____

4. You **tell** Tom about the fireworks.

_____

5. We **go** with his family.

_____

Name _____

- **Proper nouns** name specific people, places, or things.
- Proper nouns begin with a capital letter.
- Some proper nouns are the names of geographical places.

Florida	South America	Pacific Ocean
Europe	United States	California

Choose the proper noun that names a place. Write it correctly on the line below.

1. africa
land
place

_____

2. state
alaska
mountain

_____

3. rain forest
stream
cuyahoga river

_____

4. map
brazil
hill

_____

5. iowa
city
village

_____

6. lake
water
atlantic ocean

_____

7. new york
coast
waterfall

_____

8. grassland
desert
mexico

_____

Name _____

> • The irregular verbs **go, do, see, say,** and **tell** have special forms in the past tense.

Read the paragraph and circle the mistakes. Then rewrite the paragraph correctly on the lines.

Last week, I see my friend Alice outside. I say to her, "Would you like to read a book with me?" We goed back to my house. We read a book about kids in other countries. Alice telled me she would come over again.

_____
_____
_____
_____

Connect to Community Write about a disagreement between people in your community. What did the people disagree about? Tell what people said to explain why they felt as they did.

Name _____

Write the past tense of the verb in ( ) to complete each sentence.

1. We _____ a movie about children in Mexico. (see)

2. Our teacher _____ that all children like to have fun. (say)

3. _____ you meet the children from Canada? (Do)

4. They _____ to the park to learn the game. (go)

5. We _____ them how to draw the game board. (tell)

6. They _____ how we played the game. (see)

7. Jack _____ with us to teach the game. (go)

8. He _____ that everyone had fun. (say)

Look back through your writer's notebook for irregular verbs you have used. Check that you used them correctly. Fix any mistakes you find.

Name _____

Content words are words that are specific to a field of study. Words like Earth, earthquake, and volcano are science content words.

Sometimes you can figure out what a content word means by using context clues.

Go on a word hunt with a partner. Find content words related to science. Write them in the chart.

Science	
_____	_____
_____	_____
_____	_____

CONNECT TO CONTENT

"Into the Sea" gives facts about how ocean water can wash away things on land. The author uses content words that help you understand the topic.

Circle two words that you were able to figure out the meaning to using context clues. Write the words and what they mean on the lines.

_____

_____

_____

_____

Name _____

**Read the clues. Complete the puzzle with the vocabulary
words below. Use the letters in the boxes to solve the riddle.**

common	customs	earth	favorite
island	parades	understand	wonder

1. The opposite of rare ☐ _ _ _ ☐ _

2. To know what something means _ _ _ _ _ _ _ ☐ _ _

3. Habits or usual ways of doing things _ _ _☐☐ _ _

4. Best liked ☐ _ _ _ _ _ _ _

5. Marches through the streets on holidays ☐_ _☐_ _ _

6. A small bit of land surrounded by water ☐ _ _ _ _ _

7. Surprise, awe, or curiosity _ _☐_ _ _

8. Dirt, or the planet we live on _ _ _☐_

What kind of coat can you put on only when it is wet?

A ☐ ☐ ☐ ☐ ☐ ☐ ☐ ☐ ☐ ☐ ☐

Name _____

> Each syllable in a word has a vowel sound in it.

Say the picture name. Then say the syllables in the word. Draw an X in the box for each syllable you hear. Write the number of syllables on the line.

1.

_____

2.

_____

3.

_____

4.

_____

5.

_____

Teacher Directions: Model 1. *Listen as I say the first word: pencil. Say the syllables with me: pen-cil.* Model drawing 2 X's and writing the number of syllables on the line.

Name _____

Listen to the sounds your teacher says. Blend the sounds to make a word. Circle the picture that goes with the word.

Teacher Directions: Model item 1 by saying: */s/ /t/ /îr/. Listen as I blend these sounds: /ssstîr/,* steer. *I see a picture that shows someone steering, so I will circle it.* Guide children to blend the sounds and circle the picture. For items 2-5, have children listen to the sounds, blend them to form a word, and circle the correct picture. 2. /b/ /îr/ /d/ 3. /f/ /ûr/ /n/ 4. /s/ /t/ /är/ /z/ 5. /s/ /t/ /r/ /i/ /ng/

Name _____

The letters *eer* can stand for the r-controlled vowel sound you hear in *deer*.

 d<u>eer</u>

A. Read the words. Use a word from the box to complete each sentence.

career	eerie	engineer	peer
sneer	steers	deer	volunteer

1. Writing is his _____.

2. It is not nice to _____ at people.

3. She wants to work as an _____.

4. They _____ over the wall at the bird.

5. At night, the street lights look _____.

6. Mom _____ the car into the parking space.

7. The _____ ran into the forest when they saw us.

8. I like to do _____ work at the park.

Name _____

Some words have the sounds you hear at the ends of the words *deer, here*, and *smear*. The letters **eer, ere**, and **ear** can stand for this sound.

deer   here   smear

A. Use a word from the box to complete each sentence.

peering   unclear   here   cheerful   hears

1. Lance _____ birds singing.

2. The writing on the sign is _____.

3. The boys are _____ into the toy shop window.

4. We all just got _____.

5. The team was _____ when they won the game.

B. Circle the word that matches the picture and write it on the line.

6.  _____
   ear   eat   tear

7.  _____
   speak   shirt   spear

8. _____
   tears   tent   team

9. _____
   bed   beard   bead

Name _____

> An **abbreviation** is a short way to write a longer word.
>
> Titles are often abbreviated.　　　**Mr.** for **Mister**
> Places may also be abbreviated.　　**Ave.** for **Avenue**

A. Draw a line to match each word with its abbreviation.

1. Street　　　　　**a.** Rd.

2. Mount　　　　　**b.** St.

3. Apartment　　　**c.** Dr.

4. Doctor　　　　　**d.** Apt.

5. Road　　　　　　**e.** Mt.

B. Write each title or place on the line using an abbreviation.

6. Doctor Smith _____

7. Seaside Avenue _____

8. Spring Road _____

9. Apartment 7A _____

10. Mount Olympus _____

Name _____

Complete each sentence. Use the words in the box.

again	behind	eyes	gone	happened
house	inside	neither	stood	young

1. What _____ at the store today?

2. This ball is _____ mine nor yours.

3. He has brown _____ and black hair.

4. Come back _____ before it gets dark.

5. She _____ on a chair to reach the high shelf.

6. How far away is your _____ from our school?

7. My brother is too _____ to go on that ride.

8. I looked for her, but she seems to be _____ now.

9. I don't want to go back to the same place _____.

10. Don't let him fall _____ the rest of us.

Writing/Spelling Connection

Look back through your writer's notebook for places you used these high-frequency words. Check that you spelled them correctly. Fix any mistakes you find.

Name _____

Fold back the paper along the dotted line. Use the blanks to write each word as it is read aloud. When you finish the test, unfold the paper. Use the list at the right to correct any spelling mistakes.

1. _____   1. deer

2. _____   2. cheers

3. _____   3. steer

4. _____   4. here

5. _____   5. jeer

6. _____   6. near

7. _____   7. ear

8. _____   8. dear

9. _____   9. clear

10. _____   10. spear

Review Words   11. _____   11. store

12. _____   12. north

High-Frequency Words   13. _____   13. again

14. _____   14. house

15. _____   15. inside

Name _____

deer	cheers	steer	here	jeer
near	ear	dear	clear	spear

A. Look at the spelling words in the box. Match the spelling word with the vowel spelling pattern and write the word.

ear	*eer*	*ere*
1. _____	6. _____	10. _____
2. _____	7. _____	
3. _____	8. _____	
4. _____	9. _____	
5. _____		

B. A letter is missing from each spelling word below. Write the missing letter in the box. Then write the spelling word correctly on the line.

11. h ☐ re _____   12. ste ☐ r _____

13. ne ☐ r _____   14. je ☐ r _____

15 cle ☐ r _____

Name _____

deer	cheer	tear	here	peer
near	ear	dear	clear	fear

A. Look at the spelling words in the box. Match the spelling word with the vowel spelling pattern and write the word.

ear	*eer*	*ere*
1. _____	7. _____	10. _____
2. _____	8. _____	
3. _____	9. _____	
4. _____		
5. _____		
6. _____		

B. A letter is missing from each spelling word below. Write the missing letter in the box. Then write the spelling word correctly on the line.

11. h☐re _____

12. che☐r _____

13. ne☐r _____

14. de☐r _____

15. cle☐r _____

Name _____

> deer   cheery   steer   here's   jeering
> rear   nearing   dear   appeared   spears

A. Look at the spelling words in the box. Match the spelling word with the vowel spelling pattern and write the word.

ear	*eer*	*ere*
1. _____	6. _____	10. _____
2. _____	7. _____	
3. _____	8. _____	
4. _____	9. _____	
5. _____		

B. A letter is missing from each spelling word below. Write the missing letter in the box. Then write the spelling word correctly on the line.

11. h[ ]re's _____   12. ste[ ]r _____

13. ne[ ]ring _____   14. je[ ]ring _____

15. spe[ ]rs _____

Name _____

> • The **tense** of a verb tells when the action takes place.
>
> • The **progressive tense** can show an action that is, was, or will be in progress.
>
> • To form the progressive tense, use a helping verb together with a verb with the **-ing** ending.
>
> **Present:** I <u>am reading</u> that book right now.
>
> **Past:** Oscar <u>was reading</u> the book last week.
>
> **Future:** Kayla <u>will be reading</u> the book after me.

Use the tense and the verb shown to write progressive-tense sentences. Write the new sentences on the lines.

1. present: I (play) soccer after school today.

_____

2. past: Dad (help) me practice last week.

_____

3. future: My friends (form) two teams.

_____

4. present: The coach (call) to us.

_____

 Think of something you like to do. Write about it using the progressive tense. Try to include sentences for the present, the past, and the future progressive tense.

Name _____

> - The **tense** of a verb tells when the action takes place.
> - The **perfect tense** can show that an action begins and ends at different points in time.
> - To form the perfect tense, use a helping verb together with the past tense form of a verb.
>
>   **Present:** I <u>have seen</u> that film before.
>
>   **Past:** I <u>had seen</u> it with my mom last year.
>
>   **Future:** I <u>will have seen</u> it twice after today.

Use the tense and the verb shown to write sentences in the perfect tense. Write the new sentences on the lines.

1. past: My brother and I (make) a chore chart last month.

_____

2. present: We (check) the chart everyday.

_____

3. present: I (walk) the dog this morning.

_____

4. past: My brother (feed) the dog earlier.

_____

5. future: We (follow) the chart for almost a month.

_____

Name _____

> • A **contraction** is a short form of two words.
> • An **apostrophe** takes the place of the missing letter or letters when the two words are joined.

Add the apostrophe to each contraction. Write the contraction correctly on the line.

1. Walking through the snow isnt easy. _____

2. I cant see over the high wall. _____

3. We couldnt see across the street during the last storm.

_____

4. Mom wouldnt let us go out in the storm. _____

5. We shouldnt go outside until the storm ends. _____

6. I havent seen a storm like that for many years. _____

7. We dont want another one to come. _____

8. We arent ready for such cold weather. _____

Name _____

> • The **progressive tense** can show an action that is, was, or will be in progress. To form the progressive tense, use a helping verb together with a verb with the **-ing** ending.
> • The **perfect tense** can show that an action begins and ends at different points in time. To form the perfect tense, use a helping verb together with the past-tense form of a verb.

Read the paragraph and circle the mistakes in the progressive or perfect tense. Rewrite the paragraph correctly on the lines.

I is helping Dad in the yard today. We were raked leaves all morning. Mom had fixing lunch for us, so we went inside. During lunch, the wind was started to blow. It was scattered all the leaves. So, we will working again. My mom and sister is planning to help us. We are hoped to finish before dinner.

_____

_____

_____

_____

_____

Connect to Community

Think about events in your community. How do people make the events happen? How do you take part in them. Use the progressive tense to tell what happens.

Name _____

**A. Read each sentence. Underline the verb. Then write
"progressive" or perfect to name the tense.**

1. I am going berry picking with my mom tomorrow. _____

2. We are painting the kitchen this week. _____

3. Tomas and Ben have started to write their report. _____

4. My Mom will have worked at the shop for three years.

   _____

5. The scientists will be working on a cure. _____

6. My team has won three games. _____

**B. Write one progressive tense sentence and one perfect tense
sentence to tell about a past, present, or future action.**

7. _____.

8. _____

**Writing/Spelling
Connection**
Look back through your writer's notebook progressive
and perfect tense sentences you have written. Check to
see that you have used the correct form of each verb.

Name _____

> Look at this example of **context clues** in a **sentence**. The underlined words explain what *height* means.
>
> Now imagine waves that reach a height of over 100 <u>feet tall!</u>

Read each sentence. Write the meaning of the word in bold print. Underline the context clues in the sentence that helped you.

1. **Tsunamis** are a set of ocean waves that rush over land.

_____

2. One event is an undersea **earthquake** that causes the ocean floor to move and shake.

_____

3. They **extend**, or reach, deep down into the ocean.

_____

4. The waves head for **shore**, the land along the ocean.

_____

5. Tsunamis cause lots of **damage** and harm.

_____

Name _____

> **Homographs** are words that are spelled the same but have different meanings. They may sound different, or they may sound the same.

Read each sentence. Circle the definition that fits the homograph in bold print. On the line, write a sentence that uses the other definition of the word.

1. I will **lead** you to your new desk.

   the part of a pencil that you write with   to show the way

   _____

2. The **wind** blows through the trees.

   air moving in the sky   to wrap around something over and over

   _____

3. I am going to **tear** up this paper.

   a drop that falls from the eye when   to rip apart
   a person is crying

   _____

4. They will **train** him to do the job right.

   a string of cars that move on a track   to teach

   _____

Name _____

Each syllable in a word has a vowel sound in it.

Say the picture name. Then say the syllables in the word. Draw an X in the box for each syllable you hear. Write the number of syllables on the line.

1.

           _____

2.

           _____

3.

           _____

4.

           _____

5.

           _____

Teacher Directions: Model 1. *Listen as I say the first word: carrot. Say the syllables with me: car-rot.* Model drawing 2 X's and writing the number of syllables on the line.

Name _____

Look at each picture. Say the name of each picture out loud. Say the vowel sound. Place an X on the picture whose name has a different vowel sound.

1.

2.

3.

4.

5.

Teacher Directions: Model item 1 by saying *beard, board,* and *sword.* Repeat, stressing the difference between the vowel sounds. Say: *The words* board *and* sword *have the same vowel sound:* /ôr/. Beard *has a different vowel sound:* /îr/. Guide children to cross out the picture with the beard.

Name _____

When the letters ***are, air, ear,*** and ***ere*** work together, they can stand for the sounds you hear in ***mare, pair, bear,*** and ***there***. It is an *r*-controlled vowel sound.

m*are*   **p*air***    **b*ear***    **th*ere***

Find the words that complete the sentences. Write the word on the line.

repair	rare	wear	pear
share	fair	where	careful

1. Can you _____ the broken chair?

2. Mike snacks on a _____.

3. Mel and Ray _____ their toys.

4. It is _____ to see a bear.

5. We _____ hats when it is cold.

6. Meg spots a pig at the _____.

7. I don't know _____ you went.

8. Be _____ when you cross the street.

Name _____

When the letters **are**, **air**, **ear**, and **ere** work together, they can stand for the sounds you hear in **square**, **hair**, **pear**, and **there**. It is an *r*-controlled vowel sound.

squ<u>are</u>   h<u>air</u>   p<u>ear</u>   th<u>ere</u>

A. Look at each picture. Circle the word that names the picture. Write the word.

1.

_____
anywhere   artist
airplane

2.

_____
gear   glare   glory

3.

_____
scare   square   stairs

4.

_____
tearing   tired
teapot

5.

_____
share   spare   stairs

6.

_____
peach   pet   pear

B. Go back and underline the letters that stand for the vowel sound you hear in the word *air* in each answer above.

Name _____

> When a vowel or a pair of vowels is followed by the letter *r*, it changes the vowel sound. When dividing a word by syllables, the vowels and the *r* stay in the same syllable.
>
> **gar·den**   **con·cert**   **bor·der**

Write the words from the word box that have the same *r*-controlled vowel as each word listed below. Then draw lines to divide the words into syllables.

birthday	prepare	turkey	circus
forget	market	parcel	
normal	purple	careless	

1. cart _____ _____

2. fort _____ _____

3. curl _____ _____

4. dare _____ _____

5. stir _____ _____

Name _____

Complete each sentence. Use the words in the box.

among	bought	knew	never	once
soon	sorry	talk	touch	upon

1. Dinner will be ready _____.

2. He _____ a new hat at the store.

3. I have _____ heard of them before.

4. Dad likes to _____ to his friends a lot.

5. Who _____ you would like to go first?

6. We _____ you would love this place.

7. She is _____ to have knocked you down.

8. My sister will be hungry _____ we arrive.

9. She put the hat _____ the head of the snowman.

10. I am tall enough to _____ the shelf but not to reach the books on it.

Name _____

Fold back the paper along the dotted line. Use the blanks to write each word as it is read aloud. When you finish the test, unfold the paper. Use the list at the right to correct any spelling mistakes.

1. _____   1. dare

2. _____   2. stare

3. _____   3. fare

4. _____   4. hair

5. _____   5. pair

6. _____   6. chair

7. _____   7. bear

8. _____   8. pear

9. _____   9. where

10. _____   10. there

Review Words   11. _____   11. dear

12. _____   12. cheers

High-Frequency Words   13. _____   13. knew

14. _____   14. never

15. _____   15. talk

Name _____

dare	stare	fare	hair	pair
chair	bear	pear	where	there

A. Look at the spelling words in the box. Match the spelling word with the spelling pattern and write the word.

are

1. _____

2. _____

3. _____

ear

7. _____

8. _____

air

4. _____

5. _____

6. _____

ere

9. _____

10. _____

B. An extra letter has been added to each spelling word below. Draw a line through the letter that does not belong. Write the correct word on the line.

11. beare _____

12. chaier _____

13. wheare _____

14. daire _____

15. faire _____

Name _____

dare	stare	fare	stairs	pair
chair	bear	pear	where	there

A. Look at the spelling words in the box. Match the spelling word with the vowel pattern and write the word.

are

1. _____

2. _____

3. _____

air

4. _____

5. _____

6. _____

ear

7. _____

8. _____

ere

9. _____

10. _____

B. An extra letter has been added to each spelling word below. Draw a line through the letter that does not belong. Write the correct word on the line.

11. beare _____

12. chaier _____

13. wheare _____

14. daire _____

15. paire _____

Name _____

snare	stare	fare	hairless	flair
chair	wear	tear	where's	there's

A. Look at the spelling words in the box. Match the spelling word with the vowel pattern and write the word.

are

1. _____

2. _____

3. _____

air

4. _____

5. _____

6. _____

ear

7. _____

8. _____

ere

9. _____

10. _____

B. An extra letter has been added to each spelling word below. Draw a line through the letter that does not belong. Write the correct word on the line.

11. weare _____

12. chaier _____

13. wheare's _____

14. flaire _____

15. faire _____

Name _____

• A **conjunction** is a word that joins together sentences, phrases, or words. Common conjunctions are **and, but,** and **so**.

• A **compound sentence** is two simple sentences joined with a comma and a conjunction.

Carly likes dogs. Max likes cats.

Carly likes dogs, <u>but</u> Max likes cats.

Combine the two sentences. Write the new sentence on the line.

1. Mel sang a song. Pam danced.

_____

2. Mom wants to see a play. Dad wants to see a movie.

_____

3. Mike was hungry. He made a sandwich.

_____

4. Kim wrote the story. Brian drew the pictures.

_____

5. It is getting late. I will go to bed.

_____

 Write about what you and your friends do for fun. Include some compound sentences to make your sentences more interesting.

Name _____

> • You can combine two simple sentences to make a **compound sentence**.
> • Join the two sentences with a comma and a conjunction such as **and, but,** or **so**.
>
>   Liza fell down. She got back up.
>
>   Liza fell down, <u>but</u> she got back up.

Combine the two sentences. Write the new sentence on the line.

1. Carl dropped his pen. It rolled under the desk.

_____

2. I want the blue pants. They are the wrong size.

_____

3. Dad cooks dinner. We wash the dishes.

_____

4. The trash can is full. Ben takes out the trash.

_____

5. I took my book with me. I didn't read it.

_____

Name _____

> - Begin every sentence with a capital letter.
> - Use end punctuation to separate sentences and keep them from running together.
> - End a statement or a command with a period. End a question with a question mark. End an exclamation with an exclamation point.
> - Use a comma before a conjunction in a compound sentence.

Read the sentences. Write the sentences correctly on the lines.

1. what do you want to read

   _____

2. that boy likes poetry but I love a good mystery.

   _____

3. your book looks interesting tell me about it.

   _____

4. that is amazing

   _____

Connect to Community What makes your community great? Think of something you love about your community. Write about why you love it and how you think it might be made even better.

Name _____

> • You can combine two simple sentences to make a **compound sentence**.
> • Join the two sentences with a comma and a conjunction such as **and, but**, or **so**.
>
> Kevin <u>walks</u> down the street. Kat runs to catch up to him.
>
> Kevin <u>walks</u> down the street, and Kat runs to catch up to him.

Combine the two sentences. Write the new sentence on the line.

1. Pam likes hot dogs. Mike prefers hamburgers.

_____

2. Saul wants to go out. He does his homework quickly.

_____

3. Mom sings the song. Dad joins in.

_____

4. The lights went out. I grabbed my flashlight.

_____

5. My sister laughs at the joke. I don't think it is funny.

_____

 **Writing/Spelling Connection** Look back through your writer's notebook for places you could combine sentences. Use a comma and a conjunction to combine them.

Copyright © McGraw Hill. Permission is granted to reproduce for classroom use.

Name _____

You can combine two simple sentences to make a longer
sentence. Join the sentences with a comma and a conjunction,
such as **and**, **but**, or **so**.

Jill runs to hide. We will try to find her.

Jill runs to hide, and we will try to find her.

Billy liked the game. He didn't win it.

Billy liked the game, but he didn't win it.

Combine the two sentences. Write the new sentence on the line.

1. Matt didn't feel well. Mom took him to the doctor.

_____

2. The book is on the shelf. It is too high to reach.

_____

3. Jen walks the dog. Gina feeds it.

_____

4. Sara drops the ball. She picks it up again.

_____

Name _____

> **Antonyms** are words that have opposite meanings.

Read each pair of sentences. Find the two words that are antonyms. Circle the antonyms and then write them on the lines.

1. They use hot glue to keep the blocks from coming apart.
   The glue cools quickly and holds everything together.

   _____   _____

2. The workers finish the outside walls.
   Then they move to the inside walls.

   _____   _____

3. The shelf above that counter is filled with cookbooks.
   There are more books below the counter.

   _____   _____

4. When spring comes, the igloo melts.
   The people must wait until winter when the water freezes to build the next igloo.

   _____   _____

Name _____

Use a word from the box that matches the definition.

| active | explode | music | parades |
| properties | rhythm | steep | travels |

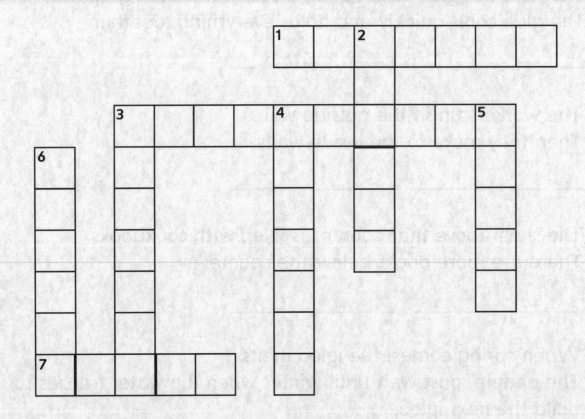

Across
1. Trips over land or water
3. Lands that are owned
7. Songs

Down
2. Moving around or doing things a lot
3. Marches through the streets for holidays
4. Blow up
5. Sharply uphill or downhill
6. The beat of a song

Name _____

Say the name of each picture. Draw lines to match the pictures that have the first and last sound reversed.

1. 

2.    

3.

4.    

5. 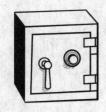   

Teacher Directions: Model item 1 by saying *net*. Have children repeat the word. Explicitly say each phoneme: /n/ /e/ /t/. Say: *I'm going to reverse the first sound, /n/, and the last sound, /t/, in the word* net: /t/ /e/ /n/. Guide children to match *net* to ten.

Name_____

Listen to the word your teacher says. Replace the sound. Circle the picture of the new word.

Teacher Directions: 1. Model Point to the picture and say: *This is a* mouse. *I can change the /m/ in* mouse *to /h/. The new word is* house. Guide children to circle the picture. Have children do the following. **2.** *rocket;* change /r/ to /l/ **3.** *crowd;* change /r/ to /l/; **4.** *clown;* change /l/ to /r/; **5.** *kitten:* change /k/ to /m/.

Name _____

Sometimes the letters **ou** and **ow** can stand for the vowel sound you hear in the words **house** and **cow**.

h<u>ou</u>se   c<u>ow</u>

A. Circle the word that names each picture. Then write the word on the line.

1.		2.		3.	
	clown		ground		toaster
	claim		grin		trick
	coal		groan		tower
_____		_____		_____	

B. Choose the words from the box to complete each sentence. Then write the words on the lines.

clouds	around	south	flowers

4. How many _____ will Jill see in the sky?

5. In the Fall, birds fly _____.

6. The store is _____ the corner.

7. We planted _____ in the garden.

Name _____

Sometimes the letters **ou** and **ow** can stand for the vowel sound you hear in the words **shout** and **clown**.

sh<u>ou</u>t   cl<u>ow</u>n

Look at each picture. Use the letter tiles to write each picture name.

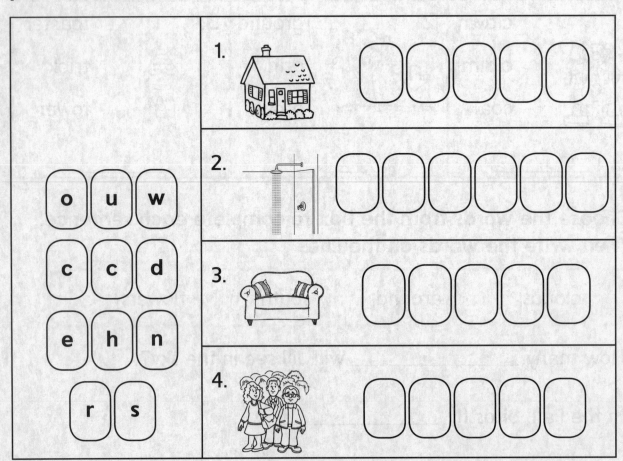

Name _____

> Some nouns change their spelling to name more than one.
>
> **man   men   child   children**
>
> Some words do not change their spelling to name more than one.
>
> **sheep   sheep**

A. Circle the correct word to complete the sentence. Write the word.

1. Jan has three pet _____.

mouses   mice

2. I got two new _____ for my tank.

fish   fishes

3. I put both my _____ into the water.

feet   foots

4. I lost five _____ last year.

teeth   tooths

5. There are twenty _____ in the race.

woman   women

B. Read the sentence. Underline the word that names more than one thing. Write the word.

6. I saw three sheep. _____

7. Many children came to the party. _____

8. There were two deer in the park. _____

Name _____

Complete each sentence. Use one of the words in the box.

answer	been	body	build	head
heard	minutes	myself	pretty	pushed

1. He put the hat on his _____.

2. I will be ready in five _____.

3. Have you _____ this story?

4. I have _____ to the creek and back.

5. She _____ the chair against the wall.

6. I walked to the park by _____.

7. The ribbons in your hair are very _____ .

8. I don't know the _____ to your question.

9. They plan to _____ a bridge over the river.

10. The human _____ can do remarkable things.

Look back through your writer's notebook for places you used these high-frequency words. Check that you spelled them correctly. Fix any mistakes you find.

Name _____

Fold back the paper along the dotted line. Use the blanks to write each word as it is read aloud. When you finish the test, unfold the paper. Use the list at the right to correct any spelling mistakes.

1. _____   1. sound

2. _____   2. mound

3. _____   3. cloud

4. _____   4. shout

5. _____   5. pound

6. _____   6. clown

7. _____   7. brown

8. _____   8. crown

9. _____   9. howl

10. _____   10. growl

Review Words   11. _____   11. chair

12. _____   12. where

High-Frequency Words   13. _____   13. been

14. _____   14. myself

15. _____   15. pushed

Name _____

sound	mound	cloud	shout	pound
clown	brown	crown	howl	growl

A. Write the spelling words that have the *ou* spelling pattern.

1. _____   2. _____

3. _____   4. _____

5. _____

B. Write the spelling words that have the *ow* spelling pattern on the line.

6. _____   7. _____

8. _____   9. _____

10. _____

C. A letter is missing from each spelling word below. Write the missing letter in the box. Then write the spelling word correctly on the line.

11. so⬜nd _____   12. clo⬜n _____

13. cl⬜ud _____   14. gro⬜l _____

15. mo⬜nd _____

Name _____

sound	ouch	cloud	loud	pound
clown	brown	cow	howl	owl

A. Write the spelling words that have the *ou* spelling pattern.

1. _____ 2. _____

3. _____ 4. _____

5. _____

B. Write the spelling words that have the *ow* spelling pattern.

6. _____ 7. _____

8. _____ 9. _____

10. _____

C. A letter is missing from each spelling word below. Write the missing letter in the box. Then write the spelling word correctly on the line.

11. so☐nd _____ 12. clo☐n _____

13. cl☐ud _____ 14. o☐l _____

15. po☐nd _____

Name _____

| wound | pouches | around | bounced | underground |
| scowling | gown | crown | howling | growling |

A. Write the spelling words that have the *ou* spelling pattern.

1. _____   2. _____

3. _____   4. _____

5. _____

B. Write the spelling words that have the *ow* spelling pattern.

6. _____   7. _____

8. _____   9. _____

10. _____

C. A letter is missing from each spelling word below. Write the missing letter in the box. Then write the spelling word correctly on the line.

11.   wo☐nd _____   12.   sco☐ling _____

13.   ar☐und _____   14.   gro☐ling _____

15.   po☐ches _____

Name _____

- A **pronoun** takes the place of one or more nouns.
- The pronouns *I, he, she, it*, and *you* are singular pronouns. They take the place of singular nouns.

    <u>Amy</u> likes to help people. <u>She</u> volunteers on Saturdays.
- Some pronouns refer to people or things that are not named.

    <u>Everything</u> is in place. <u>Nobody</u> wanted to go home.

Circle a pronoun to replace the underlined noun in each sentence.

1. <u>Sarah</u> likes to help animals.

    She   It

2. <u>Adam</u> volunteers with her at an animal shelter.

    He   It

3. <u>The shelter</u> is near their school.

    You   It

4. <u>A person</u> can help at the shelter.

    Anyone   Everything

 Use the sentences as a model. Write about someone you admire. Use pronouns to add details about why you admire this person.

Name _____

> - A **pronoun** agrees with the noun it replaces. Singular pronouns replace singular nouns.
> - A plural noun names more than one person, place, or thing.
> - The pronouns **we**, **you**, and **they** can take the place of a plural noun or a noun and a pronoun together.
>
>   <u>People</u> vote in elections. <u>They</u> vote in elections.
>   <u>Connor and I</u> are good citizens. <u>We</u> are good citizens.

Circle the correct pronoun in ( ) to complete each sentence.

1. Our class will have an election tomorrow. (We, You) will vote in the morning.

2. We will pick Jim or Sue to be the class leader. (We, They) are both good choices.

3. Sue helps clean the room after school. (It, She) is a good leader.

4. Jim and Sue are on the safety patrol. (They, You) help us stay safe.

5. Jim and Sue, thank you for leading us. (We, You) show us how to be good citizens!

6. Carrie and I will count the votes. (We, They) will count them during recess.

Connect to Community Pretend you are running for class leader. Write about why your classmates should vote for you. Use pronouns as you tell about what you will do if elected.

Name _____

> • The pronoun *I* always begins with a capital letter.
> • Use *I* as the subject of a sentence.
>   I like to play sports.

Correct the sentences and write them on the lines.

1. Bob and i are on the soccer team.

_____

2. i like working with the other children.

_____

3. i want to be a good member of the team.

_____

4. After practice, i am very tired.

_____

5. The coach and i talked about how to kick.

_____

6. My teammates and i have fun together.

_____

Name _____

> - A **pronoun** is a word that takes the place of a noun or nouns.
> - The pronouns *I*, *he*, *she*, *it*, and *you* are singular pronouns.
> - The pronouns *we*, *you*, and *they* can take the place of a plural noun or a noun and a pronoun together.

Underline each mistake. Then rewrite the paragraphs correctly on the lines below.

> Mr. Lewis asked, "How can we be good citizens?"
> Jenny raised her hand. "I think we can help other people,"
> it said.
>
> Mr. Lewis smiled. They said, "I agree with you, Jenny."
> The other children agreed. It said, "Let's make a list of ways
> to help."

_____

_____

_____

_____

_____

_____

Name _____

Mark the pronoun that could replace the underlined words.

1. <u>Erin</u> is reading to Mrs. Jackson.

    ○ They   ○ She   ○ I   ○ We

2. <u>Mrs. Jackson</u> likes it when children visit her.

    ○ She   ○ He   ○ It   ○ We

3. <u>My mother and I</u> live near Erin.

    ○ It   ○ She   ○ I   ○ We

4. <u>Tom and John</u> helped Mrs. Jackson by raking her leaves.

    ○ They   ○ She   ○ It   ○ We

5. <u>The leaves</u> fell from a big tree.

    ○ They   ○ It   ○ I   ○ We

6. <u>Tom</u> raked the leaves into a pile.

    ○ They   ○ He   ○ It   ○ We

7. <u>Mrs. Jackson</u> said, "Thank you, everyone!"

    ○ They   ○ She   ○ It   ○ We

Writing/Spelling Connection **Look back through your writer's notebook for singular and plural pronouns you have used. Check that you used them correctly. Are there places where you could replace nouns with pronouns?**

Name _____

Expand your vocabulary by adding or removing inflectional endings, prefixes, or suffixes to a base word to create different forms of a word.

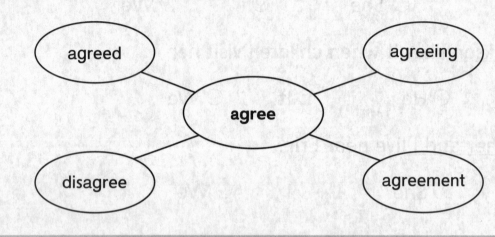

Use your notes from "César Chávez." Choose one word and write it in the word web. Add circles to the web to write as many related words as you can. Use a dictionary to help you.

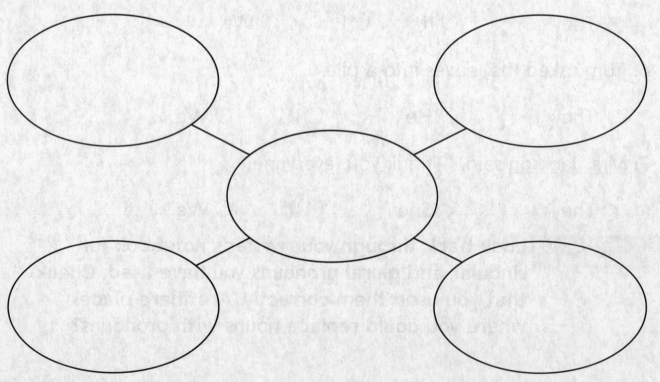

Name _____

Read the clues. Complete the puzzle with your vocabulary words. Use the letters in the boxes to solve the riddle.

drops	excite	insists	local
outdoors	pale	solid	sounds

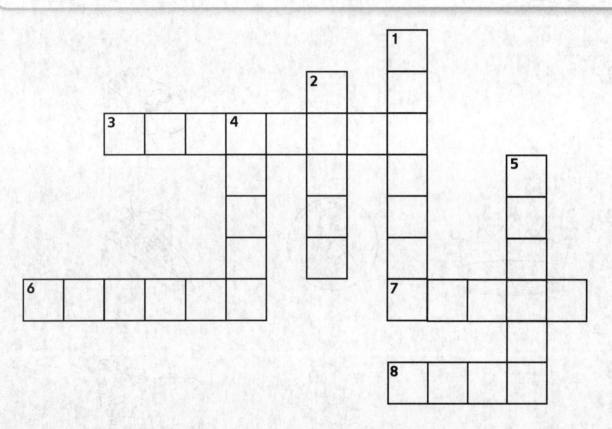

Across
3. Not inside a building
6. Noises
7. Holding a firm shape
8. Light in color

Down
1. Argues firmly
2. Nearby
4. Small beads of water
5. To stir strong feelings in

Name _____

Listen to the sounds your teacher says. Blend the sounds to make a word. Circle the picture that goes with that word.

1.

2.

3.

4.

Teacher Directions: Model item **1** by saying: */s/ /t/ /är/. Listen as I blend these sounds: /ssstär/,* star. *I see a picture that shows a star so I will circle it.* Guide children to blend the sounds and circle the picture. For items 2-5, have children listen to the sounds, blend them to form a word, and circle the correct picture. **2.** Say: /f/ /ou/ /n/ /t/ /ə/ /n/ **3.** Say: /k/ /oi/ /n/; **4.** Say: /f/ /l/ /ou/ /ər/.

Name _____

Listen to the word your teacher says. Replace the sound. Circle the picture of the new word.

1.

2.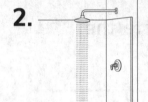

3.

4.

5.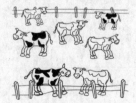

Teacher Directions: 1. Model Point to the picture and say: This is a *boy*. I can change the /b/ in *boy* to /j/. The new word is *joy*. Guide children to circle the picture. Have children do the following. **2.** *shower*; change /sh/ to /t/; **3.** *crown*; change /k/ to /f/; **4.** *tracks*; change /t/ to /c/; **5.** *mound*; change /m/ to /h/.

Name _____

> The letters *oi* and *oy* can stand for the vowel sound you hear in the words *oil* and *boy*.
>
> o<u>i</u>l   b<u>oy</u>

Circle the word that names each picture. Then write the word on the line.

1. sole / soil / sale	**2.** cone / cane / coin	**3.** voice / voted / vase
4. job / joyful / jug	**5.** boat / boil / bow	**6.** cowboy / convoy / annoy

Name _____

The letters *oi* and *oy* can stand for the sound you hear in the words ***boil*** and ***joy***.

b<u>oi</u>l   j<u>oy</u>

Look at each picture. Write the letters *oy* or *oi* to complete the picture name.

1. ch____ce	**2.**  cowb____	**3.**  n____se
4.  br____l	**5.**  p____nt	**6.**  enj____

Name _____

> When a word ends in **-le, -el,** or **-al,** the consonant before it plus the ending form the last syllable.
>
> pud/**dle**   duf/**fel**   vo/**cal**

A. Draw a line to divide each word into syllables. Write each syllable on the line.

1. puzzle _____ _____

2. purple _____ _____

3. funnel _____ _____

4. total _____ _____

5. little _____ _____

B. Use the words from section A to complete the sentences.

6. Henry used a _____ to pour the tea into a jar.

7. What is the _____ cost for all of the items?

8. Sarah finished putting the _____ together.

9. My favorite color is _____.

10. Serena held the _____ kitten in her arms.

Name _____

Complete each sentence. Use the words in the box.

brought	busy	else	happy	I'll
laugh	love	maybe	please	several

1. _____ bake cookies after dinner.

2. She is going to _____ her new bike.

3. _____ we can go to the fair tomorrow.

4. I am too _____ to go to the store today.

5. _____ be quiet while the baby is asleep.

6. They were so _____ to hear you're all right.

7. They _____ their dog with them to the park.

8. He found _____ pretty rocks at the beach.

9. Who _____ do you want to invite to the party?

10. We _____ every time we see that funny road sign.

Name _____

Fold back the paper along the dotted line. Use the blanks to write each word as it is read aloud. When you finish the test, unfold the paper. Use the list at the right to correct any spelling mistakes.

1. _____ **1.** soil

2. _____ **2.** broil

3. _____ **3.** moist

4. _____ **4.** point

5. _____ **5.** toil

6. _____ **6.** oil

7. _____ **7.** toy

8. _____ **8.** joy

9. _____ **9.** coin

10. _____ **10.** noise

Review Words

11. _____ **11.** crown

12. _____ **12.** mound

High-Frequency Words

13. _____ **13.** I'll

14. _____ **14.** laugh

15. _____ **15.** maybe

Name _____

soil	broil	moist	point	toil
oil	toy	joy	coin	noise

A. Look at the spelling words in the box. Write the spelling words that have the *oy* pattern.

1. _____ 2. _____

B. Write the spelling words that have the *oi* pattern.

3. _____ 4. _____

5. _____ 6. _____

7. _____ 8. _____

9. _____ 10. _____

C. A letter is missing from each spelling word below. Write the missing letter in the box. Then write the spelling word correctly on the line.

11. bro ☐ l _____ 12. to ☐ _____

13. m ☐ ist _____ 14. po ☐ nt _____

15. so ☐ l _____

Name _____

soil	boil	choice	point	toil
oil	toy	joy	coin	noise

A. Look at the spelling words in the box. Write the spelling words that have the *oy* pattern.

1. _____   2. _____

B. Write the spelling words that have the *oi* pattern.

3. _____   4. _____

5. _____   6. _____

7. _____   8. _____

9. _____   10. _____

C. A letter is missing from each spelling word below. Write the missing letter in the box. Then write the spelling word correctly on the line.

11. bo☐l _____   12. to☐ _____

13. ch☐ice _____   14. po☐nt _____

15. so☐l _____

Name _____

soil	broiling	moist	foil	coil
choices	pointed	coy	coins	noises

A. Look at the spelling words in the box. Write the spelling words that have the *oy* pattern.

1. _____

B. Write the spelling words that have the *oi* pattern.

2. _____   3. _____

4. _____   5. _____

6. _____   7. _____

8. _____   9. _____

10. _____

C. A letter is missing from each spelling word below. Write the missing letter in the box. Then write the spelling word correctly on the line.

11. bro ☐ ling _____   12. co ☐ _____

13. m ☐ ist _____   14. po ☐ nted _____

15. so ☐ l _____

Name _____

> • The pronouns *I* and *we* can be subjects in a sentence.
>
>   <u>I</u> like to work in a group.   <u>We</u> are meeting today.
>
> • The pronouns *me* and *us* can be used in the predicate part of the sentence.
>
>   Jake works with <u>me</u>.   He asked <u>us</u> to help.
>
> • Name yourself last when talking about yourself and another person.
>
>   Molly and <u>I</u> are writing the report.
>
> • The pronoun *I* is always a capital letter.

A. Write *I* or *me* to complete each sentence.

1. _____ am working with Tyler, Jake, and Robin.

2. Tyler asked _____ to help him with some art.

B. Write *we* or *us* to complete each sentence.

3. Liam is going to work with _____ , too.

4. _____ like his artwork.

 Use the sentences as a model. Write about a perfect day with your family. Use the pronouns *I, me, we,* and *us* to tell what you would do with your family on a perfect day and what the people in your family would do to help make your day perfect.

Name _____

- Some pronouns tell about who owns what. These are called **possessive** pronouns.
- Possessive pronouns can take the place of possessive nouns in a sentence.

  Kathy's cat = <u>her</u> cat   Billy's dog = <u>his</u> dog
  the neighbors' turtle = <u>their</u> turtle
  the bird belonging to you = <u>your</u> bird
  the hamster belonging to me = <u>my</u> hamster
  the pets belonging to us = <u>our</u> pets

On the line, write the words that can take the place of the underlined words. Use possessive pronouns in each answer.

1. <u>The cake belonging to you</u> is on the plate. _____

2. I saw <u>Mom's pen</u> on the desk. _____

3. I think <u>Dad's papers</u> were on the table. _____

4. I hung <u>the coat belonging to me</u> in the closet. _____

5. Where are <u>Jim's and Carol's</u> shoes? _____

6. Now we know where all <u>the things belonging to us</u> are.

_____

Name _____

> When you write a date, place a comma between the day of the month and the year.
>
> **I was born September 1, 2013.**
>
> If you include the day of the week, place a comma between it and the month.
>
> **Please come over Sunday, September 1.**
>
> If you continue the sentence after a date that has one or more commas in it, place a comma after the date.
>
> **I was born September 1, 2013, and so was Daniel.**
>
> **Please come over Sunday, September 1, at 2:00 p.m.**

Rewrite the sentences. Add commas where they are needed.

1. We will leave Monday July 5 and return Saturday July 10.

_____

_____

2. My parents met July 4 2006 and married July 4 2010.

_____

_____

3. We will have a party Monday July 4 2022 at this park.

_____

Name _____

> • The pronouns *I* and *we* can be used as subjects in a sentence.
>
> • The pronouns *me* and *us* can be used in the predicate part of a sentence.
>
> • The pronouns *my, our, their, your, his,* and *her* tell about who owns what.
>
> • The pronoun *I* is always a capital letter. *I* is used in the subject of a sentence.

Underline the mistakes. Rewrite the paragraph correctly on the lines.

Me wanted to build a treehouse. It was a big job. i asked Dad to help i. Him got he hammer and some wood. Us worked all day on it. At the end of the day, us were done. Their hard work paid off. Me treehouse is the best!

_____

_____

_____

_____

_____

Connect to Community   What is your personal role in your community? Write about what your community does for you and what you do in return. Use subjective, objective, and possessive pronouns.

Name _____

Write C if the underlined pronoun is correct. If the pronoun is not correct, cross it out and write the correct pronoun on the line.

1. <u>Me</u> like to make crafts with my friends. _____

2. <u>Us</u> make lots of things together. _____

3. Would you like to join <u>we</u>? _____

4. Bring <u>you</u> markers with you. _____

5. At the craft show, we will show all <u>our</u> crafts. _____

6. Can you help <u>I</u> with my craft? _____

7. I like how Nina colored on <u>she</u> craft with markers. _____

8. Beth and Nina made two of <u>they</u> crafts to match. _____

Look back through your writer's notebook for possessive pronouns you used. Check that you used them correctly.

Name _____

> **Synonyms** are words that have almost the same meaning.

Read each sentence. Write the two words that are synonyms.

1. In that time, teaching was a common occupation, or job, for women.

   _____   _____

2. Women in health care were only supposed to assist, or help, male doctors with their work.

   _____   _____

3. Elizabeth did not agree or accept that.

   _____   _____

4. Elizabeth studied and learned medicine for two years.

   _____   _____

5. She wanted sick people to have less pain and discomfort.

   _____   _____

6. The women also ran a school to train, or teach, other women as doctors.

   _____   _____

Name _____

Use this entry from an online dictionary to answer the questions.

---

parade (puh-RAYD) From Middle French, c. 1650.

noun: **1.** A march held to celebrate something, usually with a marching band.

　2. A march of soldiers for a military display.

　3. Any situation in which many people or things pass by: a *parade* of customers.

verb (paraded, parading)

verb used with object: **4.** To show something off: to *parade* your knowledge.

verb used without object: **5.** To march in a group or as if with a group: to *parade* for the Fourth of July.

　6. To march for a military display: to *parade* for the general.

---

1. What is the pronunciation of *parade*? _____

2. Where and when does the word *parade* come from?

　_____

3. What example does the dictionary give for how to use the word *parade* as a noun? _____

4. What meaning does the word *parade* have when it is a verb used with an object? _____

Name _____

Every syllable in a word must have a vowel sound.

Say the picture name. Then say each syllable in the word. Draw an X for each syllable. Write the number of syllables on the line.

1.   _____

2.   _____

3.   _____

4.   _____

Teacher Directions: Model 1. *Listen as I say the first word:* butterfly. *Say the syllables with me:* but-ər-flī. Model drawing 3 X's and writing the amount of syllables on the line.

Name _____

Say the name of each picture. Say the beginning sounds. Place an X on the picture whose name has a different beginning sound.

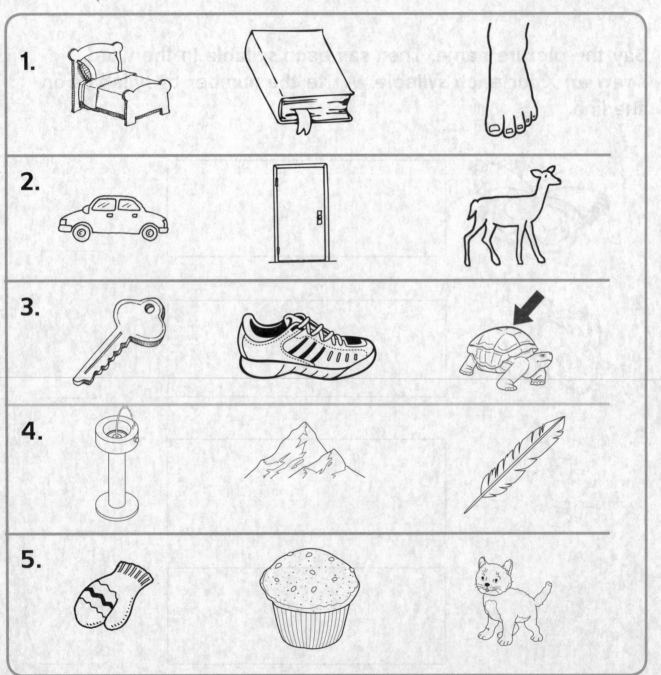

1.

2.

3.

4.

5.

Teacher Directions: 1 Model Say *bed, book, foot.* Repeat, emphasizing the beginning sounds. Say: *The words* bed *and* book *have the same beginning sound:* /b/. Foot *has a different beginning sound:* /f/. Guide children to put an X on the picture of the foot.

Name _____

> The letters **oo, u, u_e, ew, ue,** or **ui** can stand for the vowel sound you hear in the words **broom, flu, tune, drew, blue,** and **fruit**.
>
> br**oo**m t**u**n**e** dr**ew** fr**ui**t
>
> The letters **oo, ou,** or **u** can stand for the vowel sound you hear in the words **book, could,** and **bull**.
>
> b**oo**k b**u**ll

A. Read both words. Circle the word that has the vowel sound you hear in *could*. Underline the word that has the vowel sound you hear in *glue*.

1. put   tuna

2. suit   would

3. cookie   costume

B. Write *oo, ew, ue,* or *u* to complete each picture name.

4.  scr _____

5. w _____ d

6. p _____ l

7.  tiss _____

Name _____

Susan and Stuart's Book Nook

5   This bookstore is so cool!

10   Its name is "Susan and

15   Stuart's Book Nook." I look

20   at books about cooking food

25   and making fruit juice. My

31   friend Lewis pulled a book off

42   the shelf. It was about playing tunes on the flute. He

53   bought it and took it home. Lewis likes to play music.

63   My friend Drew looked at a book about making art

74   from newspapers and glue. But he put it back on the

83   shelf. Instead, he bought a book about building things

93   with wood and screws. These books are all so good!

100 We should go to this bookstore more!

1. **Circle the words that have the vowel sound you hear in** *book*.

2. **Underline the words that have the vowel sound you hear in** *cool*.

3. **Complete the sentence.**

   The bookstore's name is _____.

Name _____

A **contraction** is a short form of two words. An **apostrophe**
(') takes the place of the missing letters.

could + not = couldn't

The apostrophe (') in *couldn't* stands for the letter *o*.

**A. Read the sentences. Circle each contraction. Fill in the blanks
for the words that make up each contraction.**

1. I couldn't find my hat. _____ not

2. We shouldn't make the cake yet. should _____

3. Mom hasn't finished her work yet. _____ not

4. Dad wasn't feeling well this morning. was _____

5. They wouldn't tell me what the prize is. _____ not

B. Write the contraction for the two words.

6. would + not = _____

7. did + not = _____

8. should + not = _____

9. is + not = _____

10. do + not = _____

Name _____

Complete each sentence. Use the words in the box.

air	along	always	draw	during
ever	meant	nothing	story	strong

1. She is _____ the best at this game.

2. He likes to _____ pictures of birds.

3. Have you _____ flown on a plane?

4. I _____ to thank you for being here yesterday.

5. There is _____ I like better than roller skating.

6. Our teacher read us a _____ about two rabbits.

7. She went home _____ the break between games.

8. When Mom went to the store, I went _____ with her.

9. When Dad bakes bread, it makes the _____ smell good.

10. He is _____ enough to move that log out of the road.

Name _____

Fold back the paper along the dotted line. Use the blanks to write each word as it is read aloud. When you finish the test, unfold the paper. Use the list at the right to correct any spelling mistakes.

1. _____   1. room

2. _____   2. flu

3. _____   3. June

4. _____   4. new

5. _____   5. glue

6. _____   6. fruit

7. _____   7. crook

8. _____   8. could

9. _____   9. full

10. _____   10. push

Review Words   11. _____   11. point

                        12. _____   12. coin

High-Frequency Words 13. _____   13. along

                        14. _____   14. ever

                        15. _____   15. strong

Name _____

room	flu	June	new	glue
fruit	crook	could	full	push

A. Look at the spelling words in the box. Write the spelling words that have the vowel sound you hear in the middle of *spoon*.

1. _____ 2. _____ 3. _____

4. _____ 5. _____ 6. _____

B. Write the spelling words that have the vowel sound you hear in the middle of *book*.

7. _____   8. _____

9. _____   10. _____

C. Read each word. Write the spelling word that has the same vowel sound and vowel spelling pattern.

11. moon _____   12. suit _____

13. foot _____   14. put _____

15. blue _____

Name _____

too	flu	June	dew	clue
suit	cook	could	pull	put

A. Look at the spelling words in the box. Write the spelling words that have the vowel sound you hear in the middle of _spoon_.

1. _____   2. _____

3. _____   4. _____

5. _____   6. _____

B. Write the spelling words that have the vowel sound you hear in the middle of _book_.

7. _____   8. _____

9. _____   10. _____

C. Read each word. Write the spelling word that has the same vowel sound and vowel spelling pattern.

11. moon _____   12. fruit _____

13. foot _____   14. push _____

15. blue _____

Name _____

school	flu	June	chewed	glued
fruitcake	crooks	should	full	pushing

A. Look at the spelling words in the box. Write the spelling words that have the vowel sound you hear in the middle of *spoon*.

1. _____   2. _____

3. _____   4. _____

5. _____   6. _____

B. Write the spelling words that have the vowel sound you hear in the middle of *book*.

7. _____   8. _____

9. _____   10. _____

C. Read each word. Write the spelling word that has the same vowel sound and vowel spelling pattern.

11. moon _____   12. suit _____

13. foot _____   14. put _____

15. blue _____

Name _____

- A pronoun is a word that replaces a noun or nouns.
- A present-tense verb tells about an action that is happening right now.
- A present-tense action verb must **agree** with the subject pronoun of the sentence.
- Add *s* to most action verbs in the present tense with the pronouns *he*, *she*, and *it*.

  <u>He makes</u> rules.   <u>She votes</u> for   <u>It explains</u> the
                          the law.   rules.

Underline the verbs that agree with the subject pronouns. Write the sentences on the line.

1. She (like, likes) to think about history.

_____

2. He (thinks, think) history can teach us lessons.

_____

3. It (show, shows) us how people used to live.

_____

4. He (learn, learns) about the Constitution.

_____

 Use the sentences as a model. Write a story about two children. Use present tense and pronouns in your story. Make sure your verbs agree with their subjects.

Name _____

> • A present-tense action verb must **agree** with the subject pronoun of the sentence.
> • Add **s** to most action verbs with the singular pronouns **he**, **she**, and **it**.
>> <u>She tells</u> us about the past.
> • Do **not** add **s** to most action verbs with the pronouns **I**, **we**, **you**, and **they**.
>> <u>I see</u> a copy of the Constitution.
>> <u>You talk</u> about its importance.

Circle the verb in ( ) that agrees with the subject pronoun in each sentence.

1. We (like, likes) to visit historic places.

2. I (plan, plans) to visit the Liberty Bell.

3. They (wants, want) to see it, too.

4. She (know, knows) all about the bell.

5. You (plans, plan) to share part of the story, don't you?

6. He (reads, read) lots of books about history.

7. You (show, shows) us what our country was like long ago.

8. I (thinks, think) the bell is a special gift from the past.

Connect to Community

Write about the people in your family. What do they do? What do they like?

Name _____

> • **Proper nouns** name specific people, places, or things.
> • Proper nouns begin with a capital letter.
> • Some proper nouns are the names of people, days of week, months, locations, holidays, or schools.
>
> Jane Brown   Monday   January
> Austin, Texas   New Year's Day   Lincoln Elementary School

Choose the proper noun that names a place. Write it correctly on the line below.

1. my teacher
our dad
susan smith

_____

2. beach
countryside
atlantic ocean

_____

3. today
tuesday
yesterday

_____

4. hot season
july
summer

_____

5. hill
forest
walnut avenue

_____

6. birthday
labor day
weekend

_____

7. preschool
pratt high school
my school

_____

8. forest
falcon state park
mountain range

_____

Name _____

- Add *s* to most present-tense action verbs with the pronouns *he, she,* and *it.*
- Do **not** add *-s* to present-tense action verbs with the pronouns *I, we, you,* and *they.*

Circle the mistakes. Rewrite the paragraph correctly.

Mom and I walk to the library. She look at history books. They is her favorite kind of books. They is my favorite kind, too! I checks out a book about the Statue of Liberty. She get one about the Civil War. The books tell us about the United States. We wants to learn about American history. We thinks it is interesting.

_____

_____

_____

_____

Name _____

Underline the subject pronoun in each sentence. Then rewrite the sentence. Make the present-tense verb agree with its subject pronoun.

1. We visits a special place each year.

_____

2. They waits to see the Statue of Liberty.

_____

3. It stand tall in the harbor.

_____

4. He tell us all about the statue.

_____

5. She welcome visitors to our country.

_____

6. I wants to see it again.

_____

7. You likes studying history.

_____

8. It seem like an interesting subject.

_____

Writing/Spelling Connection

Look back through your writer's notebook for pronouns you have used. Check that you used the correct verbs with them.

Name _____

Expand your vocabulary by adding or removing inflectional endings, prefixes, or suffixes to a base word to create different forms of a word.

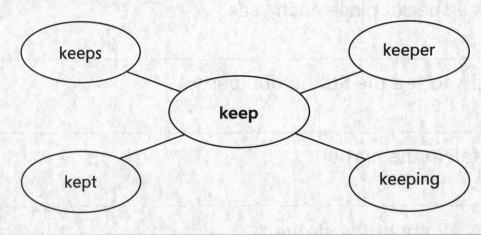

Use your notes from "A Difficult Decision." Choose one word and write it in the word web. Add circles to the web to write as many related words as you can. Use a dictionary to help you.

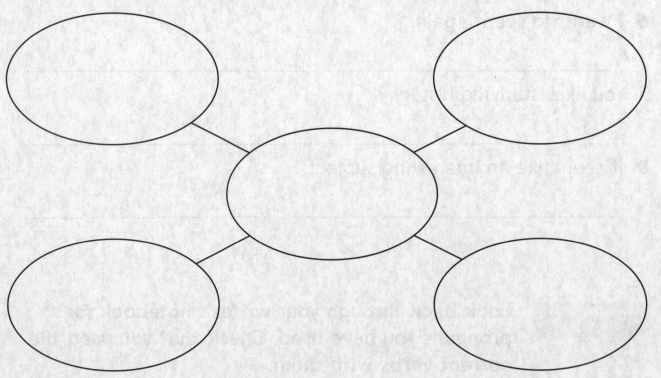

Name _____

Read the clues. Complete the puzzle with your vocabulary words. Use the letters in the boxes to solve the riddle.

agree	challenging	costume	discover
heroes	interest	study	surrounded

1. A wish to know more about ☐☐ _ _ _ _ _☐

2. People we admire ☐ _ _ _ ☐ _

3. To find ☐☐ _ ☐ _ _ _ _

4. Clothes worn to dress up as someone else _ _ _☐_ _

5. Difficult _ _ _ _ _ _ _ _☐_ _

6. Encircled _ _ _ _ _☐_☐_ _ _

7. To think alike ☐ _☐_ _

8. To try to learn about _ _ _ _☐

Where does Friday come before Thursday?

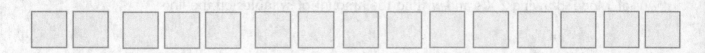

Name _____

> Every syllable in a word must have a vowel sound.

Say the picture name. Then say each syllable in the word. Draw an X for each syllable. Write the number of syllables on the line.

1.

   _____

2.

_____

3.

   _____

4.

   _____

Teacher Directions: Model 1. *Listen as I say the first word:* squirrel. *Say the syllables with me:* skwûr-əl. Model drawing 2 X's and writing the amount of syllables on the line.

Name _____

Say the first picture name. Take away the ending sound and say the new word. Circle the picture that shows it.

1.

2.

3.

4.

5.

Teacher Directions: Explain to children that we can take away a sound from a word to make a new word. **Model:** *This is* throat. *I can take away /t/ from the end of* throat *to make a new word:* throw. Guide children to circle the picture of the child throwing. Tell children to complete the other items, taking away the ending sound of the word, saying the new word, then circling the picture that shows it.

Name _____

The letters **aw, au, augh, ough, a,** and **al** can stand for the vowel sound you hear in the words **paw, haul, caught, fought, ball,** and **walk.**

p<u>aw</u>   h<u>au</u>l   f<u>ough</u>t   b<u>a</u>ll   w<u>a</u>lk

Circle the word that completes each sentence. Then write the word on the line.

1. Paul cuts wood with a _____.

sat   saw   sauce

2. We like to _____ on the phone.

tall   talk   thought

3. I gave the cat a _____ of milk.

cause   saucer   sawdust

4. My sister will _____ me in to dinner.

talk   call   chalk

5. My father _____ at this school five years ago.

brought   taught   talk

6. They _____ two tall glasses of tea to the dinner table.

drawn   brought   haunt

Name _____

The letters **aw, au, augh, ough, a,** and **al** can stand for the vowel sound you hear in the words **yawn, launch, taught, bought, tall,** and **talk**.

y<u>aw</u>n   l<u>au</u>nch   t<u>augh</u>t   t<u>a</u>ll   t<u>al</u>k

A. Look at each picture. Write aw, au, augh, ough, a, and **al to complete each picture name.**

1.   cr _____ l

2.   footb _____ ll

3.   s _____ ce

4.    j _____

5.   m _____ ll

6.    w _____ k

7.   c _____ t

8.    th _____ t

9.   h _____ l

10.   ch _____ k

Name _____

> Vowel teams are groups of vowels that make a single vowel sound, such as ***ea, ee, oa, au, ai***, and ***oo.*** A vowel and a consonant, such as ***ow, ay,*** and ***oy*** can be a vowel team, too. The letters in a vowel team stay together in the same syllable.

A. Circle the vowel team in each word. Draw a line to divide each word into syllables.

hoisting	leaving
cartoon	decay
maybe	noisy
seaside	raccoon

B. Write each word above in the correct list below.

oi	*ea*	*oo*	*ay*
_____	_____	_____	_____
_____	_____	_____	_____
_____	_____	_____	_____

Name _____

Complete each sentence. Use the words in the box.

city	father	mother	o'clock	own
questions	read	searching	sure	though

1. How many _____ are on the test?

2. My sister has a cat of her _____ now.

3. I am _____ you will have a lot of fun.

4. My brother wants to _____ that book.

5. Which _____ is the capital of our state?

6. We are _____ for the keys that Bill lost.

7. Jared has black hair like his father and _____ do.

8. Come over to my house at ten _____ in the morning.

9. Sharon's mother and _____ both work in a hospital.

10. I enjoyed the music even _____ I couldn't see the stage.

Name _____

Fold back the paper along the dotted line. Use the blanks to write each word as it is read aloud. When you finish the test, unfold the paper. Use the list at the right to correct any spelling mistakes.

1. _____
2. _____
3. _____
4. _____
5. _____
6. _____
7. _____
8. _____
9. _____
10. _____

Review Words

11. _____

12. _____

High-Frequency Words

13. _____

14. _____

15. _____

1. ball
2. small
3. paw
4. jaw
5. pause
6. sauce
7. taught
8. chalk
9. walk
10. sought
11. new
12. fruit
13. city
14. own
15. read

Name _____

ball	small	paw	jaw	pause
sauce	taught	chalk	walk	sought

A. Look at the spelling words in the box. Match each spelling word with the spelling of the vowel sound. Write the word.

      a   *aw*   *au*

1. _____   3. _____   5. _____

2. _____   4. _____   6. _____

      augh   *al*   *ough*

7. _____   8. _____   10. _____

                            9. _____

B. A letter is missing from each spelling word below. Write the missing letter in the box. Then write the spelling word correctly on the line.

11. t☐ught _____   12. wa☐k _____

13. pa☐se _____   14. ja☐ _____

15. s☐ught _____

Writing/Spelling Connection

Look back through your writer's notebook for words you used that have variant vowel /ô/ spelling patterns. Check that you spelled them correctly. Fix any mistakes you find.

Name _____

ball	mall	paw	jaw	pause
sauce	taught	chalk	walk	cough

A. Look at the spelling words in the box. Match each spelling word with the spelling of the vowel sound. Write the word.

a   *aw*   *au*

1. _____   3. _____   5. _____

2. _____   4. _____   6. _____

augh   *al*   *ough*

7. _____   8. _____   10. _____

                            9. _____

B. A letter is missing from each spelling word below. Write the missing letter in the box. Then write the spelling word correctly on the line.

11. t ☐ ught _____   12. wa ☐ k _____

13. pa ☐ se _____   14. ja ☐ _____

15. c ☐ ugh _____

Look back through your writer's notebook for words you used that have variant vowel /ô/ spelling patterns. Check that you spelled them correctly. Fix any mistakes you find.

Name _____

balls	smaller	because	caught	pause
sauce	taught	chalkboard	walked	sought

A. Look at the spelling words in the box. Match each spelling word with the spelling of the vowel sound. Write the word.

a

1. _____
2. _____

au

3. _____
4. _____
5. _____

augh

6. _____
7. _____

al

8. _____
9. _____

ough

10. _____

B. A letter is missing from each spelling word below. Write the missing letter in the box. Then write the spelling word correctly on the line.

11. t ☐ ught _____

12. wa ☐ ked _____

13. pa ☐ se _____

14. sm ☐ ller _____

15. s ☐ ught _____

Writing/Spelling Connection

Look back through your writer's notebook for words you used that have variant vowel /ô/ spelling patterns. Check that you spelled them correctly. Fix any mistakes you find.

Name _____

> - A **possessive pronoun** takes the place of a possessive noun.
> - A possessive pronoun shows who or what owns something.
> - *My*, *your*, *his*, *her*, and *its* are singular possessive pronouns.
>
>   <u>My</u> aunt is a firefighter.
>
>   <u>Her</u> job is very hard.
>
>   <u>Your</u> answer was correct.
>
>   The box was on <u>its</u> side.

Circle the correct possessive pronoun in ( ) for each sentence. Write the possessive pronoun on the line.

1. One of (my, me) favorite people in history is George Washington.

   _____

2. Mount Vernon was the name of (his, he) farm. _____

3. The farm was known for (its, he) fine house. _____

4. Martha Washington also helped (her, she) country.

   _____

5. Who is (you, your) favorite person in history? _____

 Think of something you want to own. If someone else owns it, what would you be willing to trade them for it? Use possessive pronouns to write about the trade you would offer.

Name _____

> • A **reflexive** pronoun is a pronoun that refers back to the subject of the sentence.
>
> • A reflexive pronoun ends in *-self* if the subject is singular or in *-selves* if the subject is plural.
>
> • *Myself, yourself, itself, themselves,* and *ourselves* are reflexive pronouns.
>
>   Do it <u>yourself</u>.
>
>   She fell and hurt <u>herself</u>.
>
>   The boys ate lunch by <u>themselves</u>.

Circle the correct reflexive pronoun in ( ) for each sentence. Write the reflexive pronoun on the line.

1. Chad set the table _____.

himself,   hisself

2. Sometimes I talk to _____.

myself,   myselves

3. Mary bought _____ a book.

herself,   herselves

4. We baked a cake all by _____.

ourself,   ourselves

5. Mom and Dad built this swing _____.

theirselves,   themselves

Name _____

- All of the words in a letter's **greeting** begin with a capital letter.
- Only the first word in the **closing** of a letter begins with a capital letter.
- Use a **comma** after the greeting and closing of a friendly letter.

Rewrite the letter correctly.

dear barry

    I like to read books about frogs, toads, lizards, and snakes. What do you like to read books about?

                      your friend
                      abigail

_____

_____

_____

_____

_____

Name _____

> • A possessive pronoun shows who or what owns something.
> • Some possessive pronouns are *your*, *our*, and *their*.
> • A **reflexive** pronoun refers back to the subject of the sentence.
> • Some reflexive pronouns are *yourself, ourselves,* and *themselves.*

Underline the correct possessive pronouns. Write the sentences correctly on the lines.

1. (Your, You) favorite hero is someone in your family.

   _____

2. She can tell you about her hard work (herself, herselves).

   _____

3. She works in (our, us) town's fire station.

   _____

4. She helps them fix their equipment all by (themself, themselves).

   _____

Connect to Community What can some people in your community do all by themselves? Write about some of the most impressive things that people in your community have done without any help. Use reflexive pronouns.

Name _____

Underline the possessive or reflexive pronoun that completes each sentence correctly. Write it on the line.

1. This is a story about _____ friend Jana.

   my   me   I

2. Jana was studying for a test by _____.

   her   herself   herselves

3. _____ brother Alex ran into the room.

   Her   Its   You

4. _____ eyes were big with fear.

   Its   She   His

5. "Jana, I can't do this _____," Alex said.

   me   myself   myselves

6. "Help me find _____ family's pet rabbit."

   you   they   our

7. Jana and Alex went into the yard by _____.

   theirselves   themself   themselves

8. They looked and looked until they found _____ rabbit.

   its   me   their

Look back through your writer's notebook for reflexive pronouns you have used. Fix any mistakes you find.

Name _____

> The suffixes *-tion, -sion,* and *-ion* mean "the act or result of."
>
> reflection = the act or result of reflecting

A. Underline the suffix in the word in bold print. Then write the word and its meaning.

1. I'm so glad you could help us with the **location** of our cat.

_____

2. Your **suspicion** about where he was hiding was correct.

_____

3. Asking for your help was a great **decision**.

_____

B. Use suffixes to make the correct forms of the words in ( ). Write the correct words on the lines to complete the sentences.

4. The (rebel) _____ led to the (create) _____ of a new nation.

5. She felt so much (confuse) _____ about what (act) _____ to take.

Name _____

An **idiom** is a word or a phrase that has a different meaning than the real meaning of the words.

Read each sentence. Look at the idiom in bold print.
Write the meaning of the idiom.

1. Before the talk could **get out of hand**, Mr. Webb spoke up.

   _____

2. They knew if they all **pulled together**, they could put on a great play.

   _____

3. Luz **made up her mind** that she wanted to play Henny Penny.

   _____

4. She knew the lines **by heart**.

   _____

5. When she got the part, she was so happy that she **burst into tears**.

   _____

Name _____

Say the picture name. Take away the ending sound and say the new word. Circle the picture that shows it.

1.

2

3.

4.

5.

Teacher Directions: Explain to children that we can take away a sound from a word to make a new word. **Model:** *This is* toad. *I can take away /d/ from the end of* toad *to make a new word:* toe. Guide children to circle the picture of the toe. Tell children to complete the other items, taking away the ending sound of the word, saying the new word, then circling the picture that shows it.

Name _____

Say the picture name. Then say the sounds in the word one at a time. Draw an X for each sound. Write the number of sounds on the line.

1. _____

2. _____

3. _____

4. _____

5. _____

Teacher Directions: Model 1. *I can say the sounds in the word* cloud: /k/ /l/ /ou/ /d/. Cloud *has four sounds*: /k/ /l/ /ou/ /d/. *Say the sounds with me.* Guide children to draw 4 X's and write the amount of sounds for #1.

Name _____

The short *e* sound can be spelled *ea*, as in *thread*. The short *u* sound can be spelled *ou*, as in *touch*. The short *i* sound can be spelled *y*, as in *gym*.

thr**ea**d 　　t**ou**ch 　　g**y**m

A. Underline the letters that stand for the vowel sound in each word.

double　　　spread　　　treasure　　　myth

feather　　　cousin　　　dread　　　breath

B. Circle the word that names each picture. Then write the word on the line.

1.

_____
sister　　sweater

2.

_____
young　　food

3.

_____
head　　heed

4.

_____
tiny　　gym

Name _____

> The short *e* sound can be spelled *ea*, as in *bread*. The short *u* sound can be spelled *ou*, as in *double*. The short *i* sound can be spelled *y*, as in *crystal*.
>
> bread 　　double 　　crystal

A. Read both words. Circle the word that has the short vowel sound.

1. dead   deed

2. fly   gym

3. touch   tune

4. sweet   sweat

B. Read each word. Find a word from the box that rhymes. Write the word on the line.

> symbol   sweater   young   double

1. rung _____

2. bubble _____

3. better _____

4. thimble _____

Name _____

> Words in the dictionary are listed in **alphabetical order**. This means that the words whose first letters come first in the alphabet are listed first.
>
> **apple, banana, cherry**
>
> When two words have the same first letter, the words whose second letters come first in the alphabet are listed first.
>
> **almond, apple, banana, blackberry, cashew, cherry**

A. Write the words in alphabetical order on the lines.

1. bird, bear, ape _____

2. deer, elk, donkey _____

3. slide, swings, seesaw _____

4. sand, sticks, soil _____

5. chair, bench, couch _____

6. cow, cat, dog _____

B. Write the names in alphabetical order on the lines.

7. Fred, Gloria, George _____

8. Irene, Howard, Harriet _____

9. John, Jill, Jane _____

Name _____

Complete each sentence. Use the words in the box.

| anything | children | everybody | instead | paper |
| person | voice | whole | woman | words |

1. Fold your _____ in half.

2. That _____ works at the store.

3. I have been telling _____ about this place.

4. Let's cook dinner _____ of going out to eat.

5. My sister wishes she could eat the _____ cake.

6. Lower your _____ when you are at the library.

7. The _____ in our class all enjoyed the field trip.

8. Only one _____ at a time can enter the room.

9. I can't think of the right _____ to say what I mean.

10. You must be ready for _____ when you hike in the forest.

Name _____

Fold back the paper along the dotted line. Use the blanks to write each word as it is read aloud. When you finish the test, unfold the paper. Use the list at the right to correct any spelling mistakes.

1. _____   1. dead
2. _____   2. ahead
3. _____   3. lead
4. _____   4. thread
5. _____   5. bread
6. _____   6. breath
7. _____   7. touch
8. _____   8. trouble
9. _____   9. gym
10. _____   10. myth

Review Words

11. _____   11. small
12. _____   12. chalk

High-Frequency Words

13. _____   13. instead
14. _____   14. whole
15. _____   15. words

Name _____

| dead | ahead | lead | thread | bread |
| breath | touch | trouble | gym | myth |

A. Look at the spelling words in the box.
   Write the spelling words that have the short *e* sound spelled *ea*.

1. _____   2. _____   3. _____

4. _____   5. _____   6. _____

Write the spelling words that have the short *u* sound spelled *ou*.

7. _____   8. _____

Write the spelling words that have the short *i* sound spelled *y*.

9. _____   10. _____

B. An extra letter has been added to each spelling word below. Draw a line through the letter that does not belong. Write the correct word on the line.

11. gyme _____   12. leade _____

13. deayd _____   14. mythe _____

15. threade _____

Name _____

dead	ahead	lead	tread	bread
dread	touch	trouble	gym	myth

A. Look at the spelling words in the box.
   Write the spelling words that have the short _e_ sound spelled _ea_.

1. _____   2. _____   3. _____

4. _____   5. _____   6. _____

Write the spelling words that have the short _u_ sound spelled _ou_.

7. _____   8. _____

Write the spelling words that have the short _i_ sound spelled _y_.

9. _____   10. _____

B. An extra letter has been added to each spelling word below. Draw a line through the letter that does not belong. Write the correct word on the line.

11. gyme _____   12. leade _____

13. deayd _____   14. mythe _____

15. treade _____

Name _____

dead	tread	lead	thread	breads
breathless	touches	trouble	gym	myth

C. Look at the spelling words in the box.
   Write the spelling words that have the short *e* sound spelled *ea*.

1. _____   2. _____   3. _____

4. _____   5. _____   6. _____

Write the spelling words that have the short *u* sound spelled *ou*.

7. _____   8. _____

Write the spelling words that have the short *i* sound spelled *y*.

9. _____   10. _____

D. An extra letter has been added to each spelling word below.
   Draw a line through the letter that does not belong. Write
   the correct word on the line.

11. gyme _____   12. leade _____

13. deayd _____   14. mythe _____

15. threade _____

Name _____

> • A **contraction** is a short form of two words.
> • An **apostrophe (')** shows where letters have been left out.
>
>   we are = <u>we're</u>   you are = <u>you're</u>   they are = <u>they're</u>

Write the contraction for the underlined words. Rewrite each sentence with the contraction.

1. <u>You are</u> a good worker. _____

_____

2. <u>They are</u> trying to collect old papers. _____

_____

3. <u>We are</u> going to help them. _____

_____

4. I think that <u>you are</u> very helpful. _____

_____

5. He says <u>we are</u> almost done. _____

_____

6. We will be done when <u>they are</u> all collected. _____

_____

 Use contractions to write about what the people in the room with you are doing right now. Use the sentences as a model.

Name _____

- A contraction is a short form of two words.
- An apostrophe (') shows where letters have been left out

  we have = <u>we've</u>   you had = <u>you'd</u>   she has = <u>she's</u>

Write the contraction for the underlined words. Rewrite each sentence with the contraction.

1. <u>He has</u> been looking everywhere for you. _____

   _____

2. We thought <u>you had</u> gotten lost. _____

   _____

3. <u>We have</u> been worried. _____

   _____

4. But <u>they have</u> been telling us not to worry. _____

   _____

5. They knew May was with you, and <u>she had</u> brought a map. _____

   _____

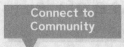
Connect to Community

What's new in your community? Write about what people have been doing lately. Use contractions.

Name _____

- Do not confuse possessive pronouns with contractions. Some sound the same but are spelled differently and have different meanings.

Possessive Pronoun	Contraction
their	they're
your	you're
its	it's

- Remember that an apostrophe takes the place of the letter or letters that are left out of a contraction.
- Possessive pronouns such as **their**, **your**, and **its** do not have apostrophes.
- Possessive pronouns tell who or what has or owns something.

Read each sentence. Circle the correct possessive pronoun or contraction. Then write it on the line.

1. (They're, Their) making posters. _____

2. (They're, Their) posters will be put on the walls. _____

3. (You're, Your) helping with the posters. _____

4. (You're, Your) poster is about saving water. _____

5. (It's, Its) a very colorful poster. _____

6. What is (it's, its) message? _____

Name _____

> • Remember that an **apostrophe** takes the place of the letter or letters left out of a contraction.
>
> • **Possessive pronouns** do not have apostrophes.

A. Draw a line below each mistake in the paragraph. Then rewrite the paragraph correctly on the lines.

Were learning about taking care of Earth. Mrs. Murphy knows a lot about Earth. Shes an expert! She says that its important to save resources. This planet is you're home. People should want they're home to be lovely for years to come!

_____

_____

_____

_____

B. Write the contractions from the paragraph above. Then write the words they stand for.

_____ = _____

_____ = _____

_____ = _____

Name _____

Underline two words in each sentence that could be used to form a contraction. Then write the contractions on the lines below.

1. We are reading a book about saving resources.

2. It is a story about real people.

3. In the story, they are living in a small town.

4. The dad is a farmer, and he is always busy.

5. The mom is a scientist, and she is fighting pollution.

6. I think that you are enjoying the story.

7. Someday I am going to save the planet.

8. Do you think that it is really possible?

1. _____   2. _____   3. _____

4. _____   5. _____   6. _____

7. _____   8. _____

Writing/Spelling Connection

Look back through your writer's notebook for contractions you have used. Check that you used them correctly. Underline any pairs of words that could be replaced with contractions.

Name _____

> **Multiple-meaning words** have more than one meaning. Use other words in the sentence to figure out which meaning is being used.

Read the lines from the poem. Circle the meaning of the word in bold print.

1. You'll never find a tortoise at sea.
   It lives on **land**—that's where it should be.

   the ground   to come down from above

2. A tortoise wears a hard outer shell
   That always works to serve it **well**.

   in a good way   a hole in the ground that stores water

3. It has four stumpy legs and four tortoise **feet**.

   measurements of 12 inches   parts of the body

4. When a tortoise doesn't know where to hide,
   It just pulls its head and four **limbs** inside.

   tree branches   legs

5. For a tortoise is a marvel of the animal **pack**.
   It carries its home right on its back.

   to put things in a suitcase   a group of animals

Name _____

Read the clues. Complete the puzzle with your vocabulary words. Use the letters in the boxes to solve the riddle.

champion	determined	Earth	perform
responsibility	rights	succeed	volunteered

1. Fair legal or moral claims _ ☐ _ _ ☐ _

2. The winner of a competition _ ☐☐ _ _ _ _ _

3. To achieve a goal ☐ _ _ _ _ _ _ _

4. The planet we live on _ ☐ _ _ ☐

5. To do, especially in front of an audience _ _ _ _ ☐ _ _

6. Offered _ _ ☐ _ _ _ ☐ _ _ _ _

7. Decided firmly _ _ _ _ _ _ _ ☐☐ _ _

8. A duty _ _ _ _ _ _ _ _ _ _ ☐ _ _ ☐ _

How can a pocket be empty but still have something in it?

☐ ☐ ☐ ☐ ☐ ☐ ☐ ☐ ☐ ☐ ☐ ☐ ☐ ☐

Name _____

> Words that rhyme end with the same sounds.
>
>

Say each picture name. Then draw two pictures of things whose names rhyme with it.

1.	
2.	
3.	
4.	

Teacher Directions: Read the box at the top of the page. Point to the pictures as you name each one: *cat, hat, acrobat.* Explain that these words rhyme. Read the directions with children.

Name _____

Listen to each word your teachers says. Add the beginning sound. Circle the picture of the new word.

1.

2.

3.

4.

5.

Teacher Directions: 1. Model *I can add sounds to words to make new words. Listen to the word* corn. *Lets add /ā/ to the beginning of* corn. *Say the new word with me.* Guide children to circle the *acorn.* **2.** Say shoe. Add /i/ to the beginning. Circle the new word. Repeat with **3.** angle, /t/; **4.** *ranch,* /b/; **5.** eagle, /b/

Name _____

> A **closed syllable** ends with a consonant. It has a short vowel sound. Some words have two closed syllables. Say **sunset**. Each syllable ends with a consonant.
>
> When a word has a blend or digraph in the middle as in **pumpkin** or **purchase**, the blend or digraph stays together. Pumpkin is divided after the *mp* blend, *pump/kin*. Purchase is divided before the *ch* digraph, *pur/chase*.
>
> An **open syllable** ends with a vowel. The vowel sound is usually long. Say **baby**. Each syllable ends with a vowel.

A. Fill in the blank with the word that completes each sentence.

> icy   dolphins   invent   reply   complete

1. I wish she would _____ to my message.

2. The sidewalk can get _____ in winter, so be careful.

3. When I grow up, I want to _____ a machine that folds clothes.

4. We watched _____ jumping out of the water.

5. I did not _____ my homework.

B. Go back and circle the open syllables in the words above. Underline the closed syllables.

Name _____

> A **closed syllable** ends with a consonant. It has a short vowel sound. When there is a blend or digraph in the middle of a word, as in **conflict** or **laughter**, the blend or digraph stays together in the same syllable. Conflict is divided before the *fl* blend, *con/flict*. Laughter is divided after the *gh* digraph, *laugh/ter*.
>
> An **open syllable** ends with a vowel. The vowel sound is usually long.

A. Read each word. Draw a line to divide each word into syllables. Then write the syllables on the lines.

secret   _____   _____

silent   _____   _____

silly   _____   _____

instead   _____   _____

B. Complete each sentence using a word from above.

1. I chose an apple _____ of a plum.

2. We have to be _____ during the movie.

3. I know what gift I will give you, but it's a _____.

4. Sometimes I like to sing _____ songs that I make up.

Name _____

A **compound word** is made up of two smaller words. Compound words have more than one syllable.

hand + made = handmade

A. Find compound words in the wordsearch.

1. _____

2. _____

3. _____

4. _____

5. _____

s	p	r	i	n	g	t	i	m	e
s	a	n	d	b	o	x	t	q	n
b	e	d	s	i	d	e	p	g	v
w	i	n	d	m	i	l	l	v	p
c	u	p	c	a	k	e	f	e	v

B. Fill in each blank with a word from above to make a compound word. Then write the compound word.

1. Kids like to play in a _____.

   _____ + _____

2. A nice time of year is _____.

   _____ + _____

3. Ted keeps his alarm clock by his _____.

   _____ + _____

4. Dad gave me a _____ to eat.

   _____ + _____

Name _____

Complete each sentence. Use the words in the box.

door	front	order	probably	remember
someone	tomorrow	what's	worry	yesterday

1. I _____ visiting this lake before.

2. Will you come to my party _____?

3. You don't need to _____ about us.

4. Where did you go on the hike _____?

5. Go see who is knocking on the _____.

6. _____ next on your list of things to buy?

7. What are you planting in the _____ yard?

8. What kind of food do you want to _____?

9. Let's find _____ who can help us lift this table.

10. We can _____ walk there in about ten minutes.

Name _____

Fold back the paper along the dotted line. Use the blanks to write each word as it is read aloud. When you finish the text, unfold the paper. Use the list at the right to correct any spelling mistakes.

Review Words

High-Frequency Words

1. _____
2. _____
3. _____
4. _____
5. _____
6. _____
7. _____
8. _____
9. _____
10. _____
11. _____
12. _____
13. _____
14. _____
15. _____

1. pencil
2. magnet
3. publish
4. supper
5. letter
6. lady
7. gravy
8. solo
9. open
10. odor
11. lead
12. touch
13. door
14. front
15. someone

Name _____

pencil	magnet	publish	supper	letter
lady	gravy	solo	open	odor

A. Write the spelling words that have a closed first syllable.

1. _____ 2. _____ 3. _____

4. _____ 5. _____

B. Write the spelling words that have an open first syllable.

6. _____ 7. _____ 8. _____

9. _____ 10. _____

C. An extra letter has been added to each spelling word below. Draw a line through the letter that does not belong. Write the correct word on the line.

11. gravvy _____   12. oppen _____

13. magnete _____   14. oddor _____

15. sollo _____

Name_____

pencil	magnet	publish	pocket	ticket
lady	gravy	solo	open	odor

A. Write the spelling words that have a closed first syllable.

1. _____   2. _____   3. _____

4. _____   5. _____

B. Write the spelling words that have an open first syllable.

6. _____   7. _____   8. _____

9. _____   10. _____

C. An extra letter has been added to each spelling word below. Draw a line through the letter that does not belong. Write the correct word on the line.

11. gravvy _____   12. oppen _____

13. magnete _____   14. oddor _____

15. sollo _____

Name _____

pencil	magnet	publish	supper	letter
lady	gravy	solo	dinosaur	crocodile

A. Write the spelling words that have a closed first syllable.

1. _____   2. _____   3. _____

4. _____   5. _____   6. _____

B. Write the spelling words that have an open first syllable.

7. _____   8. _____

9. _____   10. _____

C. An extra letter has been added to each spelling word below. Draw a line through the letter that does not belong. Write the correct word on the line.

11. gravvy _____   12. dinnosaur _____

13. magnete _____   14. crockodile _____

15. sollo _____

Name _____

> Joe's aunt grows <u>tall</u> plants.
>
> She loves the <u>yellow</u> sunflowers.

Circle each adjective and underline the noun being described.

1. Luke grows pretty flowers.

2. His garden has tall shrubs in it.

3. There are white fences.

4. Luke built wooden benches to sit on.

5. Flowers grow fast in good soil.

6. Luke plants new flowers often.

 Use the sentences as a model. Write about a place you love to visit. Use adjectives to describe the place in as much detail as you can.

Name _____

> • An **adjective** is a word that describes a noun.
> • Some adjectives tell **how many**.
>   I have many plants in my garden.
>   I picked ten green beans.

Circle each adjective and underline the noun being described.

1. We saw three rabbits in our garden.

2. Grandma planted many marigolds around the fence.

3. A bird ate six berries.

4. Ten squirrels climbed over the fence.

5. One plant had seven tomatoes.

6. I saw two butterflies on a flower.

Connect to Community Write about an important outdoor work of art in the community where you live. It could be a picture painted on a wall, or a sculpture in a park. Use adjectives to tell where it is and what it looks like.

Name _____

An **abbreviation** is a shortened form of a word. Days of the week and months of the year are often abbreviated to their first syllable. They begin with a capital letter and end with a period.

$$\text{Saturday = Sat.} \qquad\qquad \text{November = Nov.}$$

Months of five letters or fewer are usually not abbreviated.

$$\textbf{March} \qquad \textbf{April} \qquad \textbf{May} \qquad \textbf{June} \qquad \textbf{July}$$

A. Write the day of the week or month of the year that each abbreviation stands for.

1. Aug. _____

2. Mon. _____

3. Jan. _____

4. Wed. _____

5. Dec. _____

B. Write the abbreviation for each day of the week or month of the year.

6. September _____

7. Friday _____

8. February _____

9. Tuesday _____

10. October _____

Name _____

- An **adjective** is a word that describes a noun.
- Some adjectives tell what kind or how many.
- An abbreviation is a short way of writing a word. Most abbreviations begin with a capital letter and end with a period.

Read the paragraph. Underline the adjectives and circle the abbreviations. Find the mistakes. Then rewrite the paragraph correctly on the lines.

Mrs Burns and her son Tim live on Grove st. They plant white, purple, and pink flowers in their yard. They plant a big garden for berries, vegetables, and fruits. Tim works in the garden on sunny days. One days they pick fruits and vegetables from several plants. In aug. they have so many vegetables that they give some to their neighbor mr. Rojas. He invited them to his house on Sun for a delicious vegetable stew!

_____

_____

_____

_____

_____

_____

_____

Name _____

**Find the adjective and the noun it describes in each sentence.
Write them on the lines.**

1. Mr. Goff planted new plants.

   adjective _____   noun _____

2. Small birds like to fly nearby.

   adjective _____   noun _____

3. They use their long beaks to drink nectar.

   adjective _____   noun _____

4. They have built nests in the yard.

   adjective _____   noun _____

5. A large squirrel built one, too.

   adjective _____   noun _____

6. Pine trees grow quickly here.

   adjective _____   noun _____

**Writing/Spelling
Connection**

**Look back through your writer's notebook for
articles and other adjectives you have used. Check
that you used them correctly.**

Name _____

Content words are words that are specific to a field of study. Words like mammal, litter, and omnivore are science content words.

Some times you can figure out what a content word means by using context clues.

Go on a word hunt with a partner. Find content words related to money. Write them in the chart.

Money
_____ _____
_____ _____
_____ _____

CONNECT TO CONTENT

"The Life of a Dollar Bill" gives facts about what happens to dollar bills. The author uses content words that help you understand the topic.

Circle two words that you were able to figure out the meaning to using context clues. Write the words and what they mean on the lines.

_____

_____

_____

_____

Name _____

Read the clues. Complete the puzzle with your vocabulary words. Use the letters in the boxes to solve the riddle.

exclaimed	finally	form	history
issues	promises	rules	votes

1. The past _ _ _ _ _ _ ☐

2. Opinions counted when making a group decision _ ☐ _ _ _

3. Subjects to be argued about _ _ _ ☐ _ _

4. To shape _ _ ☐ _

5. At last _ _ ☐ _ _ _ _

6. Said suddenly, with emotion _ _ _ _ ☐ _ _ _ _

7. Things you have said you will do _ _ _ _ ☐ _ _ _

8. Statements about what you should and should not do

_ _ _ ☐ _

It belongs to you, but others use it more than you do. What is it?

Name_____

Listen to each word your teacher says. Add the beginning sound. Circle the picture of the new word.

Teacher Directions: 1. Model *I can add sounds to make new words. Listen to the word* two. *I can add /s/ to make the word* stew. *Say it with me.* Guide children to circle the picture. Have children do the following: **2.** Say room. Add /b/; **3.** *ants,* /p/; **4.** *ranch,* /b/; **5.** park, /s/

Name _____

Say the picture name. Then say the sounds in the word one at a time. Draw an X for each sound. Write the number of sounds on the line.

1.  _____

2. _____

3. _____

4.  _____

5. _____

6.  _____

Teacher Directions: Model 1. *I can say the sounds in the word* broom: /b/ /r/ /ü/ /m/. *The word* broom *has four sounds:* /b/ /r/ /ü/ /m/. *Say the sounds with me.* Guide children to draw 4 X's and write the amount of sounds for #1.

Name _____

> Each syllable in a word has only one vowel sound. A **final *e* syllable** ends in a vowel, consonant, final *e*. The final *e* is silent. The vowel sound before it is long. In the word ***tadpole***, the syllable ***pole*** has the long *o* sound.
>
> tad<u>pole</u>

A. Underline the final *e* syllables in the words below.

invite   mistake   female

inside   ninety   reptile

B. Choose a word from Part A that completes each sentence. Write that word on the line.

1. Meg made a _____ on her homework.

2. A snake is a _____.

3. My grandfather is _____ years old.

4. I will _____ you to my party.

5. Come _____ . It is raining.

6. My cat is not a male cat. She is a _____ cat.

Name _____

Each syllable in a word has only one vowel sound. A **final *e* syllable** ends in a vowel, consonant, final *e*. The final *e* is silent. The vowel sound before it is long. In the word ***athlete***, the syllable ***lete*** has the long *e* sound.

athl<u>ete</u>

A. Underline the final *e* syllable in each word.

perfume   reptile   excite   polite   inside   excuse

B. Circle each word in the puzzle. Look for the CVC*e* syllables to help you.

p	e	r	f	u	m	e	s	t
o	p	e	x	c	i	t	e	s
l	m	p	i	p	r	b	i	k
i	l	t	e	c	e	l	n	a
t	d	i	n	s	i	d	e	z
e	d	l	s	m	t	u	c	t
b	r	e	x	c	u	s	e	l

Name _____

> The prefix ***re-*** means "again." The prefix ***un-*** means "not." The prefix ***dis-*** means "opposite of."
>
> **reread** = read again   **untied** = not tied
>
> **dislike** = opposite of like
>
> The suffix ***-ful*** means "full of." The suffix ***-less*** means "without."
>
> **wonderful** = full of wonder   **restless** = without rest

A. Read each pair of words. Circle the word that has a prefix or a suffix. Write its meaning.

1. unhappy   usual   _____

2. cannot   careful   _____

3. disappear   downstairs   _____

4. themselves   thoughtless   _____

5. redo   river   _____

B. Read each sentence and underline the word that contains a prefix or suffix. Circle the prefix or suffix. Then write the meaning of the word on the line.

6. He feels helpless. _____

7. She and I disagree about what to do. _____

Name _____

Complete each sentence. Use one of the words in the box.

alone	became	beside	four	hello
large	notice	round	suppose	surprised

1. I _____ we'll be all right now.

2. Come sit _____ me on the couch.

3. She looked very _____ to see us.

4. You can eat the last _____ crackers.

5. Is this box _____ enough?

6. I said _____ to her when I first got home.

7. Can you draw a circle that is perfectly _____?

8. Did you _____ how happy the dog was to see Grandma?

9. He _____ very happy when we showed him his new bike.

10. This board game can be played with a friend or played _____.

Name _____

Fold back the paper along the dotted line. Use the blanks to write each word as it is read aloud. When you finish the test, unfold the paper. Use the list at the right to correct any spelling mistakes.

Review Words

High-Frequency Words

1. _____
2. _____
3. _____
4. _____
5. _____
6. _____
7. _____
8. _____
9. _____
10. _____
11. _____
12. _____
13. _____
14. _____
15. _____

1. state
2. replace
3. nine
4. ninety
5. side
6. sidewalk
7. face
8. outside
9. these
10. tadpole
11. letter
12. magnet
13. alone
14. beside
15. round

Name _____

state	replace	nine	ninety	side
sidewalk	face	outside	these	tadpole

A. Look at the spelling words in the box. Match each spelling word with the spelling of the vowel sound. Write the word.

a_e

1. _____

2. _____

3. _____

o_e

4. _____

e_e

5. _____

i_e

6. _____

7. _____

8. _____

9. _____

10. _____

B. A letter is missing from each spelling word below.

11. n☐nety _____

12. tadp☐le _____

13. outs☐de _____

14. th☐se _____

15. f☐ce _____

Writing/Spelling Connection **Look back through your writer's notebook for words you used that have CVC*e* spelling patterns. Check that you spelled them correctly. Fix any mistakes you find.**

Name _____

place	replace	nine	ninety	side
sidewalk	face	outside	pole	tadpole

A. Look at the spelling words in the box. Match each spelling word with the spelling of the vowel sound. Write the word.

a_e

1. _____

2. _____

3. _____

o_e

4. _____

5. _____

i_e

6. _____

7. _____

8. _____

9. _____

10. _____

B. A letter is missing from each spelling word below. Write the missing letter in the box. Then write the spelling word correctly on the line.

11. n☐nety _____

12. tadp☐le _____

13. outs☐de _____

14. p☐le _____

15. f☐ce _____

Writing/Spelling Connection

Look back through your writer's notebook for words you used that have CVC*e* spelling patterns. Check that you spelled them correctly. Fix any mistakes you find.

Name _____

place	replace	nine	ninety	side
sidewalk	relate	outside	compete	tadpole

A. Look at the spelling words in the box. Match each spelling word with the spelling of the vowel sound. Write the word.

a_e

1. _____

2. _____

3. _____

o_e

4. _____

e_e

5. _____

i_e

6. _____

7. _____

8. _____

9. _____

10. _____

B. A letter is missing from each spelling word below. Write the missing letter in the box. Then write the spelling word correctly on the line.

11. n☐nety _____

12. tadp☐le _____

13. outs☐de _____

14. comp☐te _____

15. rel☐te _____

Writing/Spelling Connection **Look back through your writer's notebook for words you used that have CVC*e* spelling patterns. Check that you spelled them correctly. Fix any mistakes you find.**

Name _____

- The words ***the, a,*** and ***an*** are special adjectives called **articles.**

- Use ***a*** before words that begin with a consonant sound. Use ***an*** before words that begin with a vowel sound. Both are used only with singular nouns.

- Use ***the*** with singular and plural nouns to tell about a specific thing or group of things.

    <u>a</u> car   <u>an</u> old car   <u>the</u> car over there

---

Choose the correct article in ( ).

1. I told my dad I wanted (a, an) dog.

2. He said (a, an) puppy would be too hard to take care of.

3. But he said we could get (a, an) adult dog.

4. We went to (a, the) animal shelter on Main Street to look at dogs.

5. As soon as I saw Spot, I knew she was (a, the) best dog for us.

6. She was such (a, the) happy and friendly dog.

 Use the sentences as a model. Write about what you want to be and where you want to live when you grow up. Use articles.

Name _____

- ***This, that, these,*** and ***those*** are special adjectives that tell how many and how close.
- Use ***this*** and ***that*** with singular nouns.
- Use ***these*** and ***those*** with plural nouns.

  <u>this</u> book   <u>that</u> light

  <u>these</u> wires   <u>those</u> batteries

Choose the correct adjective in ( ) to complete the sentence.

1. (This, These) solar cells will make electricity.

2. The electricity runs through (this, these) wire.

3. Carla needs (that, those) things to build a solar cell.

4. (This, These) directions show how to build it.

5. How much power will (that, those) battery hold?

6. (These, This) cell will work in bright light.

7. (This, These) video shows how it works.

8. Should I throw out (that, those) boxes?

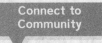
Connect to Community

What are some special places to visit in your community? Write about what makes them special. Use articles and *this, that, these,* and *those* to describe the places.

---

400   Grade 2 • Unit 6 • Week 2

Name _____

> When you write a date, place a comma between the day of the month and the year.
>
> **I was born March 1, 2013.**
>
> If you include the day of the week, place a comma between it and the month.
>
> **Please come to my party Saturday, August 1.**
>
> If you continue the sentence after a date that has one or more commas in it, place a comma after the date.
>
> **I was born March 1, 2013, on my mom's birthday.**
>
> **Please come to my party Saturday, August 1, at noon.**

Rewrite the sentences. Add commas where they are needed.

1. My mom and dad got married January 31 2010.

   _____

2. We will go camping from Friday July 31 until Tuesday August 4.

   _____

3. My brother was born July 15 2011 and my sister was born March 11 2015.

   _____

   _____

Name _____

- Use the article *a* before words that begin with a consonant sound. Use the article *an* before words that begin with a vowel sound.
- Use *that* and *this* with singular nouns. Use *these* and *those* with plural nouns.

Draw a line below each mistake in the paragraph. Then rewrite the paragraph correctly on the lines.

   I am writing an report about solar energy. It is a interesting topic. These kind of energy is made by the Sun. Solar cells change sunlight into energy. Batteries can store an energy until we need it. Mr. Ryan helped me with the report. He said solar cells work best in the sunny place like Arizona.

_____

_____

_____

_____

Name _____

A. Circle the correct word to complete each sentence.

1. Natural gas is one of (the, an) most useful fuels.

2. Natural gas can be used to heat (a, an) home.

3. It is sent through (a, an) set of underground pipes.

4. (A, An) underground pipe goes to every house where natural gas is used.

5. People in (an, the) house can stay warm all winter.

B. Circle the word that completes each sentence correctly.

6. (These, That) posters show that energy is important.

7. (This, Those) poster shows how coal is used.

8. I learned about solar energy from (that, these) pictures.

9. Show me (those, that) poster again, please.

10. (That, Those) drawings are great.

Look back through your writer's notebook for places you used articles or *this, that, these,* and *those*. Check that you used them correctly.

Name _____

> Look at this example of **context clues** in a paragraph. The underlined words help explain what the word *energy* means.
>
> We use **energy** every day to do work. With energy, <u>we can turn on a light, heat a home, cook food, and run a computer.</u>

Read each paragraph. Write the meaning of the word in bold print. Underline the context clues that helped you.

1. Yes, energy can come from the ocean. There are not many ocean power plants right now. But the ocean is a big **source** of energy.

   _____

2. The ocean has high and low **tides**. This means the water rises and falls every twelve hours. This tidal energy can be used to make power.

   _____

3. The movement of ocean waves can run a machine built to produce power. The waves move up and down inside the machine. They spin parts of the machine. The machine makes **electricity**.

   _____

4. The water temperature on the ocean's **surface** is warmer than below. That's because the sun heats the water on top. Deep below the surface, the water is very cold.

   _____

Name _____

> You can figure out the meaning of unfamiliar words by looking for **word roots**. Some English words have Greek or Latin roots.
>
> cred = to believe   spect = to look
>
> port = to carry   sta = to stand
>
> struct = to build

Read each sentence. Circle the word root in each bold print word. Then write a definition for the word.

1. The Antarctic is an **incredible** place to explore.

_____

2. One of the first jobs is to set up a research **station**, or base camp.

_____

3. Some team members **construct** the camp's buildings.

_____

4. They **transport** people and equipment to the camp.

_____

5. Some people **inspect** the camp's electricity system to make sure it is working.

Name _____

> Every syllable in a word must have a vowel sound.

Say the picture name. Then say each syllable in the word. Draw an X for each syllable. Write the number of syllables on the line.

1.   ☐ _____

2. 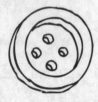 ☐ _____

3.   ☐ _____

4.   ☐ _____

5.   ☐ _____

Teacher Directions: Model 1. *Listen as I say the first word:* hamburger. *Say the syllables with me:* ham-bûr-gər. Model drawing 3 X's and writing the amount of syllables on the line.

Name _____

Say the picture name. Then say the sounds in the word one at a time. Place an X in each box for each sound you hear. Write the number of sounds on the line.

1.

_____

2.

_____

3.

_____

Listen as your teacher reads the directions.

4.

5.

Teacher Directions: Say the following sounds. Have students blend the sounds to say each word and then circle the picture that shows it. 4. /r/ /ō/ /b/ /o/ /t/; 5. /t/ /ou/ /ə / /l/

Name _____

Some words end in a consonant and *-le, -el* or *-al*. This is a final stable syllable. Listen to the ending sound in the words *candle, oval,* and *barrel*. You can hear the final stable syllable at the end of each word.

candle   o<u>val</u>   **barrel**

A. Read the words. Circle the word that names each picture. Then write the word on the line.

1.	petal pail puddle	2.	jelly juggle jiggle	3.	pickle puzzle puddle
4.	table turtle tiger	5.	call handle camel	6.	waddle wiggle whistle

Name _____

Some words end in a consonant and **-*le, -el*** or **-*al***. This is a final stable syllable. Listen to the ending sound in the words *camel, apple,* and *sandal*. You can hear the final stable syllable at the end of each word.

cam<u>el</u>    **app<u>le</u>**   **sand<u>al</u>**

Look at each picture. Write the missing letters to finish the picture name.

le   el   al

1.		shov_____	**2.**	circ_____
3.		roy_____	**4.**	tow_____
5.		beet_____	**6.**	glob_____
7.		tab_____	**8.**	nick_____

Name _____

A **contraction** is a short form of two words. An **apostrophe** (') takes the place of the missing letters.

   it + is = it's   she + has = she's   let + us = let's

A **possessive** is a word that shows who possesses, or has, something. An apostrophe (') and then an *s* are added to a singular noun to show that it possesses something. An apostrophe (') is added after the *s* of a plural noun ending in *s* to show that more than one possess something.

   the dog's leash   **the boys' project**

   Dan's party   **the girls' school**

A. Read the paragraph. Circle each contraction. Underline each possessive.

   It's almost time for Dan's party. Let's wrap this present for him. He's going to love it! We'll bring it to the Johnsons' house at 2:00. I want to watch Dan open your other friends' presents for him, too. He's been so excited about getting to open presents.

B. Look at the words you circled above. Write the words that each contraction stands for.

_____

_____

_____

_____

_____

Name _____

Complete each sentence. Use one of the words in the box.

above	brother	follow	listen	month
soft	something	song	who's	wind

1. This blanket is very _____.

2. Please _____ to me for a minute.

3. The _____ blew my hat off my head.

4. We sang a _____ around the campfire.

5. If you lead the way, we will all _____ you.

6. The flour is on the shelf _____ the spices.

7. My older _____ can help you fix your bike.

8. Do you know _____ going to be at the party?

9. We are planning to go camping next _____.

10. He is afraid he might forget to bring _____ he needs.

Name _____

Fold back the paper along the dotted line. Use the blanks to write each word as it is read aloud. When you finish the text, unfold the paper. Use the list at the right to correct any spelling mistakes.

1. _____   **1.** lit

2. _____   **2.** little

3. _____   **3.** set

4. _____   **4.** settle

5. _____   **5.** rip

6. _____   **6.** ripple

7. _____   **7.** pad

8. _____   **8.** paddle

9. _____   **9.** middle

10. _____   **10.** bubble

Review Words   11. _____   **11.** outside

12. _____   **12.** replace

High-Frequency Words   13. _____   **13.** follow

14. _____   **14.** listen

15. _____   **15.** something

Name _____

lit   little   set   settle   rip
ripple   pad   paddle   middle   bubble

A. Look at the spelling words in the box. Write the spelling words that have one syllable.

1. _____   3. _____

2. _____   4. _____

B. Write the spelling words that have a consonant plus *le* syllable.

5. _____   7. _____   9. _____

6. _____   8. _____   10. _____

C. Read each group of words. Circle the word that does not fit the pattern.

11. rip, paddle, lit   14. middle, bubble, set

12. settle, pad, rip   15. ripple, lit, settle

13. little, ripple, pad

Name _____

lit	little	set	settle	rip
ripple	pad	paddle	mid	middle

A. Look at the spelling words in the box. Write the spelling words that have one syllable.

1. _____ 3. _____ 5. _____

2. _____ 4. _____

B. Write the spelling words that have a consonant plus -*le* syllable.

6. _____ 8. _____ 10. _____

7. _____ 9. _____

C. Read each group of words. Circle the word that does not fit the pattern.

11. rip   paddle   lit

12. middle   little   set

13. settle   pad   rip

14. ripple   mid   settle

15. little   ripple   pad

Name _____

circle	little	gentle	settle	drizzle
ripple	uncle	paddle	middle	bubble

A. An extra letter has been added to each spelling word below. Draw a line through the letter that does not belong. Write the correct spelling word on the line.

1. boubble _____

2. settlle _____

3. genntle _____

4. paiddle _____

5. unckle _____

6. circkle _____

7. drizzele _____

8. ripplle _____

9. liettle _____

10. mieddle _____

B. Write a spelling word that rhymes with each word below.

11. stubble _____

12. saddle _____

13. kettle _____

14. triple _____

15. brittle _____

Name _____

> • You can use **adjectives** to compare people, places, or things.
> • Add **-er** to an adjective to compare two nouns.
>   Our team is <u>larger</u> than their team.

Underline the adjective that compares in each sentence. Write it on the lines.

1. Tim is stronger than Evan. _____

2. Julie is faster than Adam. _____

3. Soccer is a harder game than baseball. _____

4. Our field is smaller than your field. _____

5. Today's practice will be longer than yesterday's practice.
_____

6. The soccer team's shirts are brighter than the football team's shirts. _____

 Write about the people in your family. How are they different from each other and from you? Use adjectives that compare to tell how people are different.

Name _____

- You can use **adjectives** to compare people, places, and things.
- Add **-est** to an adjective to compare more than two nouns.

    Jean wants to climb the <u>tallest</u> mountain.

- For an adjective that ends in a vowel followed by a consonant, double the consonant and add **-est**.

    Tom and Tyra wore the <u>reddest</u> shirts.

- For an adjective that ends in **-e**, drop the **e** and add **-est**.

    We saw the <u>whitest</u> clouds and the <u>bluest</u> sky.

- For an adjective that ends in **-y**, change the **y** to **i** and add **-est**.

    James saw the <u>prettiest</u> bird.

Underline the adjective that compares in each sentence. Write it on the lines.

1. Lorna has the biggest backpack. _____

2. Dad will carry the heaviest tent. _____

3. This is the warmest coat I have ever worn! _____

4. The cutest squirrel ran past us on the trail. _____

5. Are you the youngest person to reach the top? _____

Name _____

> • Use an **apostrophe (')** in a contraction to show that letters have been left out.
>
>   The laptop <u>didn't </u>work.
>
> • Add an apostrophe and **s** to make a singular noun possessive.
> • Add an apostrophe to most plural nouns to make them possessive.
>
>   The <u>teacher's</u> laptop is fixed.
>
>   The <u>teachers'</u> machines are fixed.

Find the mistakes. Write the sentences correctly on the lines.

1. The two boys job is to make a video.

_____

2. That girls camera is in the box.

_____

3. A writers script needed some changes.

_____

4. One directors idea was to add a song.

_____

5. The six singers voices sounded great!

_____

Name _____

> • Add *-er* to an adjective to compare two nouns.
> • Add *-est* to an adjective to compare more than two nouns.

Draw a line below each mistake in the paragraph. Then rewrite the paragraph correctly on the lines.

Hannah's idea was to start a class newspaper. James and Kara were the better in the class at taking pictures, so they would take pictures for the newspaper. Hannah and Raj would write the stories. James and Kara thought that taking pictures would be slowest than writing. They found out something different. Taking the pictures was the fast of all the jobs.

_____

_____

_____

_____

_____

Connect to Community — **What would you like your community to be the best at? Would you rather it have the oldest buildings or the tallest buildings? The prettiest parks or the safest parks? Use adjectives that compare to write about your hopes for your community.**

Name _____

Mark the adjective that completes each sentence correctly.

1. Our group had a _____ task than the other groups.

   ○ hardest   ○ harder

2. We had to make a model of the _____ animal in the world.

   ○ biggest   ○ bigger

3. A blue whale is _____ than any other animal.

   ○ biggest   ○ bigger

4. Our teacher let us use the _____ table in the room.

   ○ larger   ○ largest

5. Mary wanted the paint to look _____ than the blue in the picture.

   ○ brighter   ○ brightest

6. Our second sketch was _____ than the first one.

   ○ nicer   ○ nicest

7. We thought our whale was the _____ animal in the class.

   ○ finer   ○ finest

Writing/Spelling Connection
Look back through your writer's notebook for adjectives that compare. Check that you used them correctly.

Name _____

Expand your vocabulary by adding or removing inflectional endings, prefixes, or suffixes to a base word to create different forms of a word.

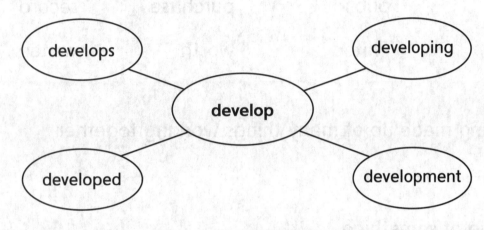

Use your notes from "Starry Asters." Choose one word and write it in the word web. Add circles to the web to write as many related words as you can. Use a dictionary to help you.

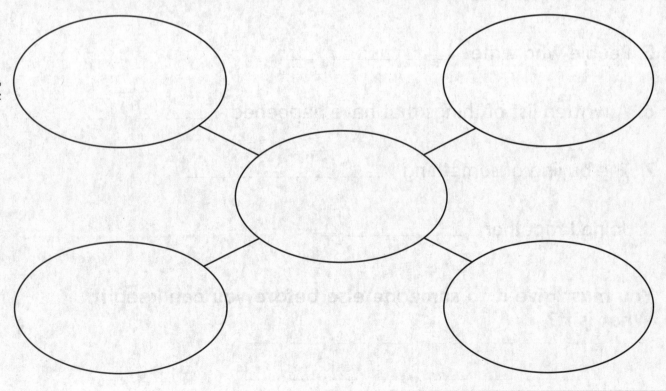

Name _____

Read the clues. Complete the puzzle with your vocabulary words. Use the letters in the boxes to solve the riddle.

prices	public	purchase	record
system	united	worth	writers

1. Something made up of many things working together

   ☐ _ _ _ _ _

2. The value of something _ ☐ _ _ _

3. Of a whole community _ ☐ _ _ _ _

4. Costs _ ☐ _ _ _ _

5. People who write ☐ _ _ _ _ _ _

6. A written list of things that have happened _ _ _ ☐ _ _

7. The buying of something _ _ ☐ _ _ _ _ _

8. Joined together _ _ _ _ _ ☐

You must give it to someone else before you can keep it. What is it?

☐ ☐ ☐ ☐ ☐ ☐ ☐ ☐

Name _____

Listen to the word your teacher says. Change the sound. Circle the picture of the new word.

Teacher Directions: 1. Model Point to the picture and say: This is a log. I can change the /o/ in *log* to /e/. The new word is *leg.* Guide children to circle the picture. Have children do the following. **2.** *tip;* change /i/ to / ī / **3.** *sticks;* change /i/ to /a/. **4.** *moose;* change /ü/ to /ou/; **5.** *streak;* change /ē/ to /ī/.

Name _____

Say the name of the first picture in each row. Circle the picture that has the first and last sound reversed.

1.

2.

3.

4.

5.

Teacher Directions: Model item 1 by saying *nap*. Have children repeat the word. Explicitly say each phoneme: /n/ /a/ /p/. Say: *I'm going to reverse the first sound, /n/, and the last sound, /p/, in the word* nap: /p/ /a/ /n/. Guide children to match *nap* to *pan*.

Name _____

When two vowels appear together in a long word, they often stay in the same syllable. This is called a **vowel-team syllable.** Listen to the vowel sounds in *cooking.*

Sometimes a vowel and a consonant can stand for one vowel sound. This is also a vowel-team syllable. Listen to the vowel sounds in *bowtie.*

c<u>oo</u>king   b<u>ow</u>t<u>ie</u>

A. Look at each picture. Write the picture name on the line.

outlaw   toenail   raincoat   beaver   window   pillow

1.   _____

2. 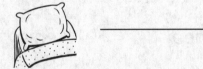   _____

3.   _____

4.   _____

5.   _____

6.   _____

B. Draw a line to divide the two syllables of each word you chose.

Name _____

> When two vowels appear together in a long word, they often stay in the same syllable. This is called a **vowel-team syllable**. Some words have a vowel team in only one syllable of the word. Listen to the vowel sounds in *hockey* and *mushroom*.
>
> **hockey**   **mushr<u>oo</u>m**

A. Write the missing letters to complete each picture name.

1. coff _____

3. birthd _____

2. classr _____ m

4. p _____ nuts

B. Write the word that completes each sentence.

| yellow | freedom | oatmeal | enjoy |

1. He did _____ that good meal.

2. We have _____ for breakfast.

3. She put her _____ raincoat away.

4. We must be brave to defend our _____.

Name _____

The *-er* ending is added to the end of a word to compare two nouns. The *-est* ending is added to the end of a word to compare more than two nouns. Some words need spelling changes first:

- if a word ends in *y*, change the *y* to *i*: dry   dr**ier**   dr**iest**
- if a word ends in *e*, drop the *e*: lat**e**   lat**er**   lat**est**
- if a word ends in a vowel and a consonant, double the final consonant: ho**t**   ho**tter**   ho**ttest**

A. Add the *-er* or *-est* ending to the word in parentheses to correctly complete the sentence.

1. I had the (lazy) day. _____

2. The (fat) pig will win the prize. _____

3. Bill had the (large) backpack. _____

4. Tina told a (funny) joke than mine. _____

5. Pam is (brave) than I will ever be. _____

B. Circle the word in each sentence that has the *-er* or *-est* ending. Write the root word on the line.

6. This is the easiest job of all. _____

7. Is this pumpkin bigger than that one? _____

8. This snack is healthier than that snack. _____

Name _____

Complete each sentence. Use the words in the box.

against	anymore	complete	enough	river
rough	sometimes	stranger	terrible	window

1. My homework is almost _____ now.

2. I propped the boards _____ the tree.

3. We walked on a trail along the _____.

4. The tree bark feels _____ when I touch it.

5. My friends and I _____ ride our bikes together.

6. The woman outside is a _____, not our neighbor.

7. Did you get _____ water, or do you want more?

8. They don't want to play with the toy robot _____.

9. It would have been _____ if we had lost our dog.

10. If you open the _____, you can hear the birds singing.

Writing/Spelling Connection **Look back through your writer's notebook for places you used these high-frequency words. Check that you spelled them correctly. Fix any mistakes you find.**

Name _____

Fold back the paper along the dottedline. Use the blanks to write each word as it is read aloud. When you finish the test, unfold the paper. Use the list at the right to correct any spelling mistakes.

1. _____

2. _____

3. _____

4. _____

5. _____

6. _____

7. _____

8. _____

9. _____

10. _____

Review Words   11. _____

12. _____

High-Frequency Words   13. _____

14. _____

15. _____

1. way

2. away

3. root

4. balloon

5. play

6. display

7. reach

8. enjoy

9. explain

10. meadow

11. little

12. middle

13. complete

14. enough

15. river

Name _____

way	away	root	balloon	play
display	reach	enjoy	explain	meadow

A. Look at the spelling words in the box. Write the spelling words that have one syllable.

1. _____   3. _____

2. _____   4. _____

B. Write the spelling words that have two syllables.

5. _____   8. _____

6. _____   9. _____

7. _____   10. _____

C. Write a spelling word that rhymes with each word below.

11. boot _____

12. contain _____

13. beach _____

14. moon _____

15. annoy _____

Name _____

> | way | away | root | balloon | play |
> |---|---|---|---|---|
> | display | reach | enjoy | plain | explain |

A. Look at the spelling words in the box. Write the spelling words that have one syllable.

1. _____   4. _____

2. _____   5. _____

3. _____

B. Write the spelling words that have two syllables.

6. _____   9. _____

7. _____   10. _____

8. _____

C. Write a spelling word that rhymes with each word below.

11. boot _____

12. contain _____

13. beach _____

14. moon _____

15. annoy _____

Name _____

repeat	away	ball	balloon	play
display	raccoon	enjoy	explain	meadow

A. Look at the spelling words in the box. Write the spelling words that have one syllable.

1. _____   2. _____

B. Write the spelling words that have two syllables.

3. _____   7. _____

4. _____   8. _____

5. _____   9. _____

6. _____   10. _____

C. Write a spelling word that rhymes with each word below.

11. greet _____

12. contain _____

13. hello _____

14. moon _____

15. annoy _____

Name _____

• An **adverb** tells more about a verb. Some adverbs tell *how* about the verb. Many adverbs end in *-ly*.

   The little boy played <u>happily</u> with the blocks.

   The banker <u>slowly</u> counted the bills.

Circle the verb in each sentence. Then write the adverb on the line.

1. The banker spoke clearly. _____

2. Charlie listened carefully. _____

3. The wind blew suddenly. _____

4. The money fell quietly. _____

5. Mary quickly answered the phone. _____

6. The children shouted loudly with joy. _____

7. My brother eagerly opened the book. _____

8. My sister skillfully climbed the tree. _____

 Write about what the people around you are doing right now. Use adverbs to tell how they are behaving.

Name _____

- An **adverb** tells more about a verb. Some adverbs tell *when* or *where* about the verb.
- Many adverbs end in *-ly*, but some do not.

    He stepped <u>inside</u>.

    A coin collector visited our class <u>yesterday</u>.

Circle the adverb in each sentence. Then underline the verb it tells about.

1. Mr. Jiminez visited our class today.

2. He sells coins nearby.

3. He told stories first.

4. Next, he showed us some coins.

5. He came here to talk to our class because his son goes to our school.

6. We all crowded forward to see the coins close up.

7. When we went outside for recess, we could not stop talking about his coins.

Connect to Community

How do people in your community feel about the different tasks they do? Write about some tasks that are done in your community. Use adverbs to tell how people behave and feel when they do these tasks.

Name _____

> • The names of special people and places are **proper nouns** and begin with a capital letter.
> • The abbreviations of **titles** before people's names begin with a capital letter. They end with a period.
>
> | | |
> |---|---|
> | Texas | Dr. Sando |
> | Canada | Ms. Oza |

Rewrite the sentences. Write the proper nouns and titles correctly.

1. A large power plant is in new york.

_____

2. The plant is near Niagara falls.

_____

3. I met dr flint when I visited the plant.

_____

4. She works at the power plant near buffalo with mr swan.

_____

5. Homes in pennsylvania use electricity from the plant.

_____

Name _____

- An **adverb** tells more about a verb. Adverbs tell *how, when,* or *where* about the verb. Many adverbs end in *-ly*.

  She moved <u>suddenly</u>.   He was here <u>yesterday.</u>

- An **adjective** is a word that describes a noun. Some adjectives tell *what kind* or *how many*.

  <u>red</u> bricks   <u>three</u> houses

Tell whether the underlined word is an adjective or an adverb.

1. Dancers moved <u>slowly</u> to the stage. _____

2. The <u>slow</u> dance began with a drumbeat. _____

3. John had a <u>surprising</u> part. _____

4. The girl moved <u>surprisingly</u> fast. _____

5. His <u>entire</u> dance was made up. _____

6. The children were <u>entirely</u> amazed by the show. _____

7. An <u>unusual</u> song began. _____

8. The horn was <u>unusually</u> loud. _____

9. John sang <u>beautifully</u>. _____

10. The costumes were <u>beautiful</u>. _____

Name _____

A. Circle the adverb in each sentence.

1. Today, we use paper money and coins.

2. I spend my money carefully.

3. My favorite store has opened nearby.

4. I can buy nice things there.

5. I happily bought some toys.

6. I go to the store early.

B. On the line, write the word in ( ) that correctly completes each sentence. The first word in ( ) is an adjective, and the second word in ( ) is an adverb.

7. He sang (clear, clearly) so we could understand the words.

   _____

8. We were (complete, completely) amazed by his singing.

   _____

9. He (careful, carefully) explained the music. _____

10. He heard the (rapid, rapidly) taps on the drum. _____

11. The (loud, loudly) note surprised us. _____

12. The musicians were smiling (happy, happily) at the end.

   _____

Writing/Spelling Connection

Look back through your writer's notebook for adverbs you have used. Check that you used them correctly. Fix any mistakes you find.

Name _____

> An **idiom** is a word or phrase that has a different meaning
> than the real meaning of the words. For example, if you hear
> that a group of people "bit off more than they could chew,"
> it probably doesn't refer to the way they eat. Rather, it means
> they have taken on a task that is too large for them to finish.

A. Read each sentence. Circle the idiom. Then write the meaning of the idiom on the line.

1. I looked outside and saw that it's raining cats and dogs.

_____

2. Now that you've said all that to him, the ball is in his court.

_____

3. We know you really wanted that toy, but it costs an arm and a leg.

_____

4. I have no power over that problem, so you're barking up the wrong tree.

_____

B. Write an ending for the sentence to show a way to use the idiom.

5. We bit off more than we could chew when we _____

_____

Name _____

> You can figure out the meaning of unfamiliar words by looking for **word roots.** Some English words have Greek or Latin roots.
>
> micro = tiny   scope = see
>
> phon = sound   tele = far away
>
> tract = pull

Read each sentence. Circle one or more word roots in each bold print word. Then write a definition for the word.

1. I talked to my uncle on the **telephone.**

_____

2. Mom looked at the stars through her **telescope.**

_____

3. The doctor looked at germs under a **microscope.**

_____

4. My cousin drives a **tractor** on a farm.

_____

5. Marie says she first felt **attracted** to Lee when they sang together.

_____

Name_____

Listen to each word your teacher says. Add the beginning sound. Circle the picture of the new word.

Teacher Directions: 1 Model: I *can add sounds to words to make new words. Listen to the word* motion. *I can add the /ē/ sound to the beginning to make the new word* emotion. Say the new word with me. Have children circle the picture that shows *emotion*. **2.** Say *glue*. Add /i/ to the *beginning. Circle the new word.* Repeat with **3.** *dress, /a/;* **4.** *under, /th/;* **5.** *ending, /b/*

Name _____

Listen to the word your teacher says. Replace the sound. Circle the picture of the new word you made.

1.

2.

3.

4.

5.

Teacher Directions: 1. Model: Point to the picture and say: The word is *work*. I can change the /k/ sound at the end to a /m/ to make a new word. The new word is *worm*. Guide children to say the word and circle the picture. Have them do the following. **2.** *splash;* change /sh/ to /t/. **3.** *streak;* change /k/ to /m/ **4.** *strike;* change /k/ to /p/ **5.** *braid;* change /d/ to /n/.

Name _____

When a vowel or a pair of vowels is followed by the letter *r*, it changes the vowel sound. The vowels and the *r* stay in the same syllable. This is called an **r-controlled syllable**. You hear *r* -controlled syllables at the end of **_under_** and the beginning of **_circus_**.

un**der**   cir**cus**

A. Connect the two syllables to make a word. Write the word on the line.

1. hor   net   _____

2. star   light   _____

3. num   ber   _____

4. per   fect   _____

B. Use the words to complete the sentences.

| border   spider   garden   turtle |

5. We grew carrots in the school _____.

6. I watched the _____ crawl up the wall.

7. Alana drew a pretty _____ around her picture.

8. The _____ sat on a log in the pond.

Name _____

When a vowel or a pair of vowels is followed by the letter *r*, it changes the vowel sound. The vowels and the *r* stay in the same syllable. You can hear **r-controlled syllables** at the end of *flow<u>er</u>* and the beginning of *<u>ar</u>tist*.

flow<u>er</u>   **<u>ar</u>tist**

Circle the words with *r*-controlled syllables. Then find them in the puzzle below.

quarter	credit	outlaw
carton	market	rulebook
lady	forget	tardy

q	u	a	r	t	e	r
m	n	t	s	k	f	o
a	c	a	r	t	o	n
r	u	r	s	t	r	i
k	c	d	a	i	g	n
e	o	y	g	j	e	e
t	s	q	i	h	t	p

Name _____

A **syllable** is a word part. Every syllable has a vowel sound. Words can have one or more **syllables**.

bas + ket + ball = 3 syllables

A. Say each word. Write 2, 3, or 4 next to the word to tell how many syllables it has.

Example: sister   2

1. horizon _____

2. understanding _____

3. equipment _____

4. impossible _____

5. banana _____

B. Fill in each blank with the word from above that best completes the sentence.

6. I like to eat a _____ with my lunch.

7. We watched the sun set on the _____ .

8. It is not _____ to run a mile if you practice.

9. We saw lots of fire _____ at the firehouse.

10. Tim is _____ the game a lot better now.

Name _____

Complete each sentence. Use the words in the box.

afternoon	ahead	anyone	everything	pretended
scientist	somehow	throughout	trouble	wherever

1. I haven't seen _____ else here yet.

2. We are going to the fair this _____.

3. My mom is a _____ who studies rocks.

4. Mom doesn't want us to run too far _____ of her.

5. Our cat and dog caused a lot of _____ together.

6. Our cat kept meowing all _____ the visit to the vet.

7. _____ you end up going, call us when you get there.

8. We packed _____ we will need in our picnic basket.

9. If we all work together, _____ we will solve the puzzle.

10. My friend _____ to cook dinner in the toy oven, but it was only toy food.

Name _____

Fold back the paper along the dotted line. Use the blanks to write each word as it is read aloud. When you finish the text, unfold the paper. Use the list at the right to correct any spelling mistakes.

1. _____   1. jumper

2. _____   2. higher

3. _____   3. star

4. _____   4. starry

5. _____   5. garden

6. _____   6. better

7. _____   7. dinner

8. _____   8. doctor

9. _____   9. market

10. _____   10. hairy

Review Words

11. _____   11. enjoy

12. _____   12. display

High-Frequency Words

13. _____   13. afternoon

14. _____   14. anyone

15. _____   15. everything

Name _____

jumper	higher	star	starry	garden
better	dinner	doctor	market	hairy

A. Look at the spelling words in the box. Match each word to the _r_-controlled vowel syllable in the word. Then write the spelling words on the lines.

_er_　　　　　　　　**_ar_**　　　　　　　　**_air_**

1. _____　5. _____　9. _____

2. _____　6. _____　　　　_or_

3. _____　7. _____　10. _____

4. _____　8. _____

B. Write the missing letter in the box. Then write the spelling word correctly on the line.

11. m☐rket _____　16. bett☐r _____

12. high☐r _____　17. doct☐r _____

13. st☐rry _____　18. dinn☐r _____

14. ha☐ry _____　19. st☐r _____

15. jump☐r _____　20. g☐rden _____

Name _____

| jumper | higher | star | stars | garden |
| better | dinner | doctor | market | hair |

A. Look at the spelling words in the box. Match each word to the *r*-controlled vowel syllable in the word. Then write the spelling words on the lines.

er   *ar*   *air*

1. _____   5. _____   9. _____

2. _____   6. _____   *or*

3. _____   7. _____   10. _____

4. _____   8. _____

B. Write the missing letter in the box. Then write the spelling word correctly on the line.

11. m ☐ rket _____   16. bett ☐ r _____

12. high ☐ r _____   17. doct ☐ r _____

13. st ☐ rs _____   18. dinn ☐ r _____

14. ha ☐ r _____   19. st ☐ r _____

15. jump ☐ r _____   20. g ☐ rden _____

Name _____

jumper	higher	stars	starry	garden
better	dinner	doctor	market	hairy

A. Look at the spelling words in the box. Match each word to the *r*-controlled vowel syllable in the word. Then write the spelling words on the lines.

er	*ar*	*air*
1. _____	5. _____	9. _____
2. _____	6. _____	*or*
3. _____	7. _____	10. _____
4. _____	8. _____	

B. Write the missing letter in the box. Then write the spelling word correctly on the line.

11. m☐rket _____

12. high☐r _____

13. st☐rry _____

14. ha☐ry _____

15. jump☐r _____

16. bett☐r _____

17. doct☐r _____

18. dinn☐r _____

19. st☐rs _____

20. g☐rden _____

Name _____

- A preposition comes before a noun or a pronoun. Some prepositions are *in, about, at, from, on, under, with, to,* and *by*.
- A prepositional phrase is a group of words that begins with a preposition and ends with a noun or a pronoun.

  He talked <u>with me</u>.
- A prepositional phrase can tell more about a noun.

  The apple tree <u>by the sidewalk</u> has ripe apples.
- A prepositional phrase can tell more about a verb.

  She saved money <u>by sticking to her budget.</u>

Underline the prepositional phrase. Circle the preposition.

1. Dad and I walked to the park.

2. Dad played catch with me.

3. I threw the ball back to him.

4. We walked on a trail.

5. We read the signs by the trail.

6. The bench under the tree is new.

7. The park by the river is my favorite place.

 Use the sentences as a model. Write about your school playground. Use prepositional phrases to tell where things on the playground are located, what you use them for, and who you use them with.

Name_____

> • A preposition comes before a noun or a pronoun. Some prepositions are *out, off, up, before, near, across, for,* and *of.*
>
> • A prepositional phrase is a group of words that begins with a preposition and ends with a noun or a pronoun.
>
> • A prepositional phrase can tell more about a noun.
>   The house <u>across the street</u> has a swing set.
>
> • A prepositional phrase can tell more about a verb.
>   We walked <u>across the street</u> to join our friends.

Underline the prepositional phrase. Circle the preposition.

1. Before dinner we will visit the pond.

2. For many years, she has collected coins.

3. The bench near the tree is painted green.

4. I brought a big bag of green apples to share.

5. He looked out the window to see who was there.

6. The squirrel grabbed the nut and ran up the tree.

7. Take the cushions off the couch so we can build a fort.

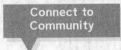 **Connect to Community**
What kinds of foods are eaten in your community? Use prepositional phrases to write about what you might see on a table at a community dinner. Tell what each food is served in or on and what it is eaten with.

Name _____

> • Use quotation marks to enclose the exact words from an author or source.
>
> • When a quote follows a tag, such as *states* and *says,* use a comma after the tag and begin the quote with a capital letter.
>
> • Use a lowercase letter for quotes that do not follow tags or are incomplete sentences.
>
> • Include end punctuation inside the quotation marks.
>
>   The author states that "fresh fruits taste best."
>
>   In Source 3, the author states, "Florida exports more grapefruits than any other place in the world."

Read the sentences. Write the sentences and quotes correctly.

1. the author states that half an alligator's length is its tail

_____

2. the author says some humming birds weigh less than a penny

_____

3. the author writes no two tigers have the exact same stripes

_____

4. the author explains that bats are the only mammals that fly

_____

Name _____

> • A preposition comes before a noun or a pronoun. Some prepositions are *down, after, since, without, during, until, between,* and *except.*
>
> • A prepositional phrase is a group of words that begins with a preposition and ends with a noun or a pronoun.
>
> • A prepositional phrase can tell more about a noun.
>   The store <u>down the road</u> is closed today.
>
> • A prepositional phrase can tell more about a verb.
>   We walked <u>down the road</u> this morning.

Underline the prepositional phrase. Circle the preposition.

1. Until lunch, we will read quietly.

2. After dinner, we will eat the cake.

3. I can't go outside without my coat.

4. I haven't seen Lisa since this morning.

5. Everyone except us is already indoors.

6. Mom and Dad put a swing between the trees.

7. Be quiet during the movie so everyone can hear.

Writing/Spelling Connection

Look back through your writer's notebook for prepositional phrases you have used. Check that you used them correctly.

Name _____

> - A preposition comes before a noun or a pronoun. Some prepositions are ***against, around, behind, beneath, beside, toward, into,*** and ***through.***
> - A prepositional phrase is a group of words that begins with a preposition and ends with a noun or a pronoun.
> - A prepositional phrase can tell more about a noun.
>   The neighbors <u>around the corner</u> are planting flowers.
> - A prepositional phrase can tell more about a verb.
>   We walked <u>around the corner</u> to the bus stop.

Underline the prepositional phrase. Circle the preposition.

1. The book is beneath Mom's purse.

2. Come sit beside me and eat dinner.

3. I propped the rake against the apple tree.

4. Paula threw the ball toward me, and I caught it.

5. The cat ran behind the couch when you arrived.

6. The dog went into its doghouse because it is cold.

7. I like to walk through the tunnel because it is cool and shady.

Name _____

A **metaphor** compares two different things, but it does not use the word *like* or *as*.

Read the lines. Write the two things the author compares. Then explain what each metaphor means.

1. The children were an army of ants, walking to class in a happy trance.

   What two things are compared? _____

   Both things _____.

2. My legs were a machine, moving me to the finish line.

   What two things are compared? _____

   Both things _____.

3. His smile was sunlight that lit up the room.

   What two things are compared? _____

   Both things _____.

4. The runner was lightning in the race.

   What two things are compared? _____

   Both things _____.

Name _____

Read the clues. Complete the puzzle with your vocabulary words. Use the letters in the boxes to solve the riddle.

appeared	crops	develop	money
rustled	shining	stages	value

1. Made soft sounds such as pages turning ☐ _ _ _ _ _ _

2. Glowing _ ☐☐ _ ☐ _

3. What you pay for things with _ ☐ _ _ _

4. Plants grown to eat or sell ☐ _ _ _ _

5. What something is worth _ _ _ _ ☐

6. Showed up _ _ _ _ ☐ _ _

7. To grow or expand _ _ _ _ _ ☐ _

8. Steps in a process _ _ _ _ _ ☐

What has a horn but does not honk?

A ☐☐☐☐☐☐☐☐☐☐

Table of Contents

Name _____

Handwriting Position

Left-Handed Writers

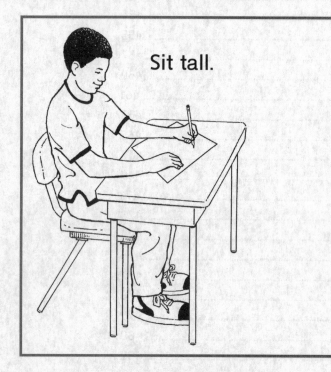

Sit tall.

Right-Handed Writers

Sit tall.

Left-Handed Writers

Look at the picture.
Hold your pencil like this.

Slant your paper like this.

Right-Handed Writers

Look at the picture.
Hold your pencil like this.

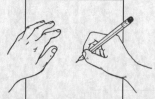

Hold your paper like this.

Name _____

Circle the letters you use to write your first name.

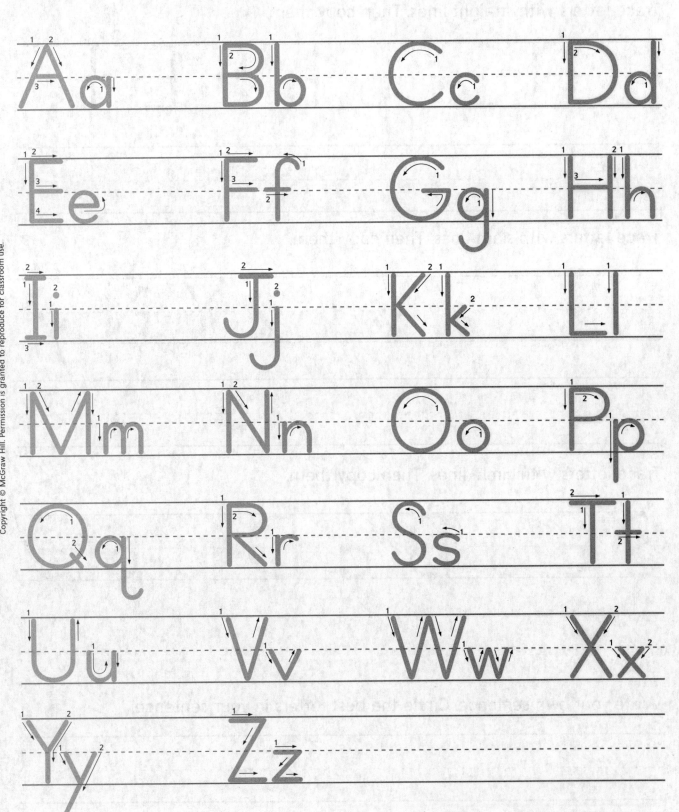

Name _____

All Kinds of Lines

Trace letters with straight lines. Then copy them.

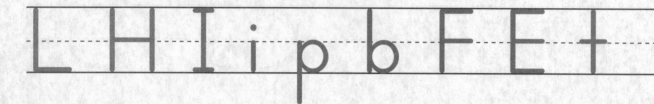

Trace letters with slant lines. Then copy them.

Trace letters with circle lines. Then copy them.

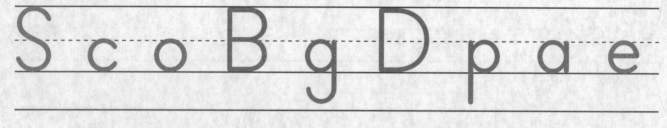

Write your own sentence. Circle the best letters in your sentence.

_____

_____

Name _____

Trace and write the letters.

Name _____

Trace and write the words and the sentence.

lit   it   ill

Lili   till   it   lit

I lit it.

Name _____

Trace and write the letters.

F   F

f   f

E   E

e   e

H   H

h   h

Name _____

Trace and write the words and the sentence.

eel   feet   teeth

Tillie   he   fell

Lili felt the eel.

Name _____

Trace and write the letters.

Name _____

Trace and write the words and the sentence.

Coco colt feel

tooth hold code

Cloe did feel cold.

Name _____

Trace and write the letters.

Q   Q

q   q

P   P

p   p

U   U

u   u

Name _____

Trace and write the words and the sentence.

Utah soup quiet

full pet lost

The pup quit it.

Name _____

Trace and write the letters.

B B

b b

J J

j j

G G

g g

Name _____

Trace and write the words and the sentence.

got jet Bobbie

Jill jog giggle

Jill got the globe.

Name _____

Trace and write the letters.

R R

r r

S S

s s

Name _____

Trace and write the words and the sentence.

rode   does   best

test   steer   frost

Lela goes to the
store.

Name _____

Trace and write the letters.

A A

a a

V V

v v

N N

n n

Name _____

Trace and write the words and the sentence.

van   Nan   Vinnie

rang   stand   have

Nan and Vinnie

sang.

Name _____

Trace and write the letters.

K   K

k   k

X   X

x   x

W   W

w   w

Name _____

Trace and write the words and the sentence.

kite   rock   fox

Willie   Xenia   wax

Wanda packed a
box.

Name _____

Trace and write the letters.

M M

m m

Y Y

y y

Z Z

z z

Name _____

Trace and write the words and the sentence.

yard yolk Maria

zebra many dizzy

Zach scored a goal.

Name _____

Numerals

Trace and write the numerals.

1

6

2

7

3

8

4

9

5

10

Write your own addition sentence.

$1 + 1 = 2$

Write your own subtraction sentence.

$2 - 1 = 1$

Name _____

Trace the punctuation marks. Write the punctuation marks and the sentences. Finish the last sentence.

.   ,   ?   !   ?   !

Who is it?

I lost my hat!

Wow,

Name _____

These words are just right.

I like to write.

The letters are not too close.
The letters are not too far apart.

Writing is fun.

There is a pencil space between words.

Write the words.

great brother

some yard pluck

Name _____

Write the sentences.

You can write a

whole sentence.

We like to read

your stories.

Name_____

Write the abbreviations.

Mr. Ms. Jr. Dr.

St. Rd. Ave. Ct.

Sept. Oct. Nov.

T. J. C. B. K. P.

Name _____

Use your best handwriting. Fill in the form.

Contact Form

Name _____

Street Address _____

City _____

State _____

Zip Code _____

Name _____

Make a poster for the Plant-a-Tree Club. Write the information.

Plant a tree. Help Earth!

Join the Plant-a-Tree Club!

Contact: (Write your phone number.)

Name _____

Complete the poem by writing the rhyming words. Then write a title at the top.

_____

- -

She's a tiny bee.
Her hive's in a

- -

Buzz! she sings,
As she flaps her

- -

Name _____

Work, little bee!
Make honey for

I like how you hum.

Your honey makes
me say,

Name _____

Copy the story onto the facing page.

Our class
visited Taos, New
Mexico, and went
rafting. Quickly,
we zoomed down
the Rio Grande. It
was great fun!

Name